11/89

D1164991

THE GIRL SCOUTS

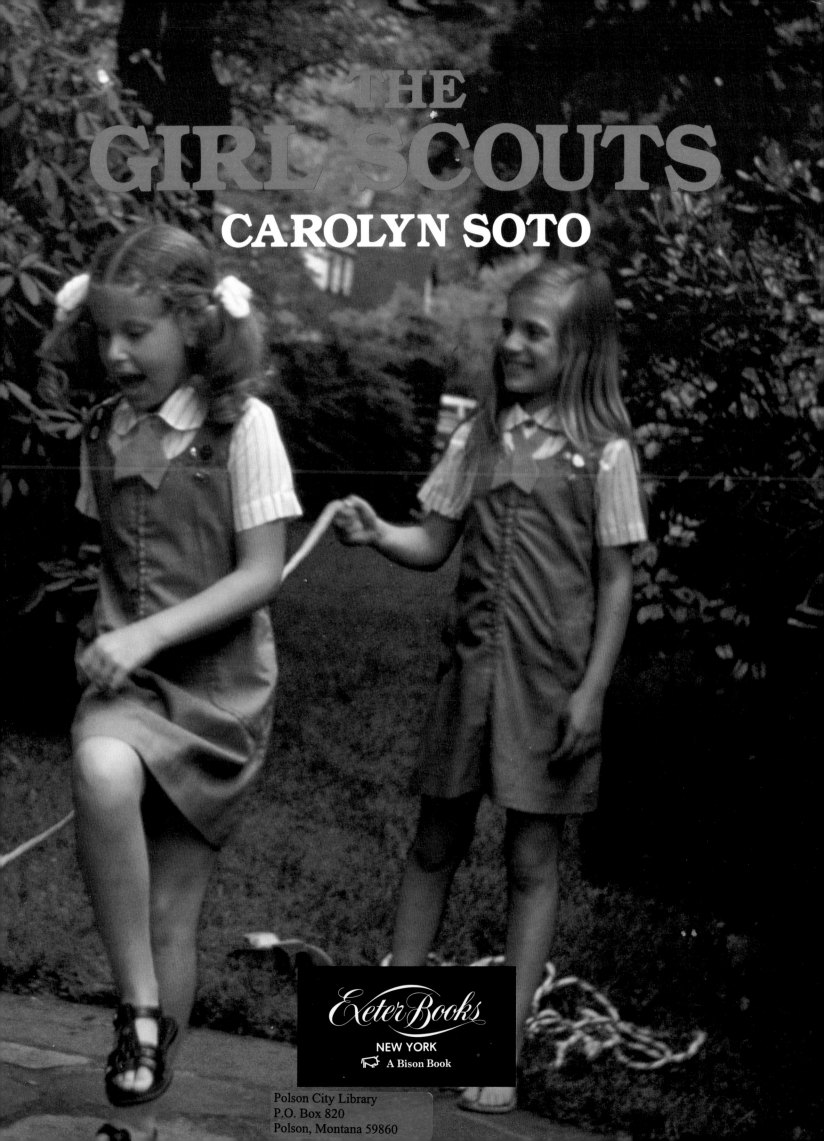

THE GIRL SCOUTS

CAROLYN SOTO

Exeter Books

NEW YORK
A Bison Book

Edited by Timothy Jacobs and John Kirk
Designed by Ruth DeJauregui and Cindy Swanson

Page 1: Daisy Scouts and an adult Scout leader explore this rock in what will become, in later Scouting experience, the World of the Out-of-Doors.

Pages 2-3: The first 'hop' is across the 'bridge' from Daisies to Brownies, who are shown here in that classic game of girlhood co-operation—jump rope!

This page: These Brownies play the game of 'Simon says.' Games, group projects and the Scouting 'worlds of interest' are enjoyable and nurturing experiences for Brownies.

CONTENTS

WORLD-WIDE GIRL SCOUTING

The international sisterhood of Girl Guides and Girl Scouts encompasses members in 108 countries. Girls of all races and religions are united by their shared ideals of good citizenship, reverence for God, and expectations of high personal ethics. Members in countries far separated by distance and customs may never meet each other and may speak different languages, but each in her own country provides similar service to others and regards the Scout or Guide Promise and Law as a life guide. Likewise, each tries to develop herself to her fullest potential, has fun in the process and believes in the strength of world friendship.

Girls voluntarily join the Girl Guides and Girl Scouts and enjoy the benefits of membership independent from political influence and control. The character guidance that Girl Guide and Girl Scout programs provide, sustains itself through successive generations of young women throughout the world, who reaffirm their commitment to Guiding and Scouting by becoming volunteer leaders or by contributing in other ways as adults.

The Girl Guides originated from the Boy Scouts and, therefore, their early history is one. Boy Scouting owes its origin to Robert Baden-Powell.

Robert Baden-Powell had the idea to train men in scouting when he was a British army officer. In 1899 he wrote a handbook for soldiers about survival in the field called *Aids to Scouting for N-COs and Men.* A woman named Charlotte Mason, who founded a college for training women teachers, was so impressed with Baden-Powell's book that she used it as one of her texts.

Also adopting the text, although unofficially, were numbers of young boys who were fascinated by the idea of being scouts. They were members of Lord Edward Cecil's Cadet Corps, formed during the Boer War in South Africa to do such responsible work during the war as carrying messages and supplies, and acting as look-outs. Mafeking was a town in South Africa that was set up by Robert Baden-Powell as the supply headquarters for the British. During the famous 217-day Siege of Mafeking, Robert

Baden-Powell led his 800 men (aided by the Cadet Corps) against 9000 Boers. When he was finally relieved from the siege by the arrival of British troops he became a famous man, the 'Hero of Mafeking.' In 1900 he became the youngest Major-General in the army, and retired from the army in 1906.

In 1907 Baden-Powell, or 'BP' as he was called, decided to hold an experimental camp, using his military training methods, for boys from different social backgrounds. This was the famous camp held at Brownsea Island in Poole Harbour. The camp was such a success that Baden-Powell rewrote his army handbook, called it *Scouting for Boys,* and published it in 1908. The Boy Scouts was born.

Baden-Powell discovered a year later that girls also were eager to become Scouts. It was at a 1909 Boy Scout rally at the Crystal Palace in London that Baden-Powell saw a group of girls wearing the shirts and hats of the boys'

Right: **Robert and Olave Baden-Powell pause during a stroll, in this 1912 photograph taken shortly after their marriage.** *Left:* **Girl Scouts and Girl Guides of the US, Denmark, Ecuador, Portugal and Bolivia were photographed in this gathering at the United Nations building in New York City.**

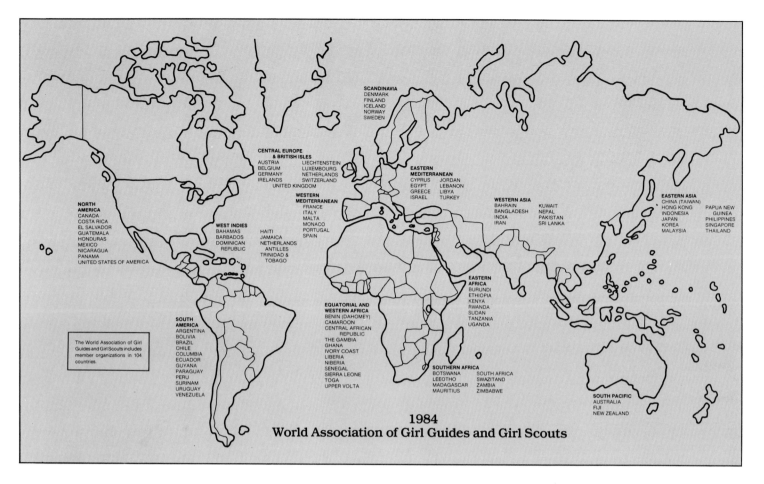

SCANDINAVIA
DENMARK
FINLAND
ICELAND
NORWAY
SWEDEN

CENTRAL EUROPE
& BRITISH ISLES
AUSTRIA   LIECHTENSTEIN
BELGIUM   LUXEMBOURG
GERMANY   NETHERLANDS
IRELANDS   SWITZERLAND
          UNITED KINGDOM

EASTERN
MEDITERRANEAN
CYPRUS   JORDAN
EGYPT   LEBANON
GREECE   LIBYA
ISRAEL   TURKEY

WESTERN ASIA
BAHRAIN   KUWAIT
BANGLADESH   NEPAL
INDIA   PAKISTAN
IRAN   SRI LANKA

EASTERN ASIA
CHINA (TAIWAN)
HONG KONG   PAPUA NEW
INDONESIA   GUINEA
JAPAN   PHILIPPINES
KOREA   SINGAPORE
MALAYSIA   THAILAND

NORTH
AMERICA
CANADA
COSTA RICA
EL SALVADOR
GUATEMALA
HONDURAS
MEXICO
NICARAGUA
PANAMA
UNITED STATES OF AMERICA

WEST INDIES
BAHAMAS
BARBADOS
DOMINICAN
REPUBLIC

HAITI
JAMAICA
NETHERLANDS
ANTILLES
TRINIDAD &
TOBAGO

WESTERN
MEDITERRANEAN
FRANCE
ITALY
MALTA
MONACO
PORTUGAL
SPAIN

EASTERN
AFRICA
BURUNDI
ETHIOPIA
KENYA
RWANDA
SUDAN
TANZANIA
UGANDA

The World Association of Girl
Guides and Girl Scouts includes
member organizations in 104
countries.

SOUTH
AMERICA
ARGENTINA
BOLIVIA
BRAZIL
CHILE
COLUMBIA
ECUADOR
GUYANA
PARAGUAY
PERU
SURINAM
URUGUAY
VENEZUELA

EQUATORIAL AND
WESTERN AFRICA
BENIN (DAHOMEY)
CAMAROON
CENTRAL AFRICAN
  REPUBLIC
THE GAMBIA
GHANA
IVORY COAST
LIBERIA
NIBERIA
SENEGAL
SIERRA LEONE
TOGA
UPPER VOLTA

SOUTHERN AFRICA
BOTSWANA   SOUTH AFRICA
LEEOTHO   SWAZITAND
MADAGASCAR   ZAMBIA
MAURITIUS   ZIMBABWE

SOUTH PACIFIC
AUSTRALIA
FIJI
NEW ZEALAND

1984
World Association of Girl Guides and Girl Scouts

The extensive global area shown *above* represents the World Association of Girl Guides and Girl Scouts, and is further unified by its individual members' 'Thinking Day' good will meditations. The Girl Guides/Girl Scouts World Centers are located in (*left to right*) Mexico, England, Switzerland and India. *At right:* Olave Baden-Powell was thought in 1914 to be 'too young' to be a help for the Girl Guides. But as of this 1919 photo, she had become the Chief Guide and the Chief Commissioner for Guides, following the hard-working example of founder Agnes Baden-Powell, BP's sister. The pendant Olave wears is the Silver Fish Award, the highest given by the UK Girl Guides.

uniforms. Instead of trousers the girls wore long blue skirts, and marched in formation behind the boys. When he asked the girls who they were, they replied, 'We're the girl scouts.' They had read *Scouting for Boys* and enacted its principles on their own. Baden-Powell could see immediately that girls were determined not to be left out of the Scouting movement and decided that they should have their own organization.

He asked his sister Agnes to help him organize Scouting for girls that very year. In 1910 the 'girl scouts' officially became the Girl Guides Association, with Agnes Baden-Powell as president. Agnes was no mere figurehead. She took to the idea of Girl Guiding with enthusiasm equal to her brother's for Boy Scouting. Agnes began to write training pamphlets and a weekly paper called 'Home Notes' for Girl Guides.

In 1912 Agnes published her brother's rewritten version of *Scouting for Boys* called *How Girls Can Help to Build Up the Empire.* In this book Baden-Powell referred to the membership as 'Guides' rather than 'Scouts,' but still included some of the same activities he had suggested for the Boy Scouts—knot tying, first aid, mapping, signaling and campfire cooking.

The general public was dubious of the Girl Guides at first. Agnes was instrumental in bringing other women

into the Girl Guide movement by encouraging them to become 'officers.' In this way some organization and respectability was introduced to the numerous groups of girls springing up around the country and calling themselves Girl Guides. Girl Guides were able to show their worth during the 1914–1918 War. One day after the declaration of war, they held an emergency meeting to discuss how they could help. To help the war effort, they did the *expected* 'women's work' (nursing troops, and knitting and sewing for them) and also the *unexpected* (running canteens and rest centers, doing laundry for hospitals, looking after children of working mothers, delivering messages, gardening and poultry farming, making sandbags and even driving ambulances—an astonishing achievement for women in 1914). By the end of the war the Guides had proved themselves loyal and capable citizens, and had earned the respect of the public.

Olave St Clair Soames married Robert Baden-Powell in 1912 at the age of 17. When she first offered her services to the Girl Guide Association in 1914, she was thought to be 'too young.' In 1916, however, she was appointed County Commissioner for Guides in Sussex and toured England with her husband in support of the Scout and Guide movements. From that time on, Lady Baden-Powell traveled extensively all over the world in the name of the Girl Guide movement. By 1923 she had travelled from Britain to North America where she made her first radio broadcast. Throughout her long life, Olave Baden-Powell was dedicated to her mission of bringing Girl Guiding to all girls. She died in 1977, 36 years after her husband. Her last message was addressed to:

'Dear Guides, Scouts, Cubs and Brownies and all their leaders and friends:

I shall have left this world when you receive this message, which I leave to express my thanks for all the kind-

GIRL SCOUTS OF THE USA PROFICIENCY BADGES

Dabbler
Child Care
Community Health and Safety
Exploring Foods
First Aid
Group Sports
Healthy Eating
Hobbies and Pets
Home Living
Household Whiz
Sports Sampler
Tending Toddlers
Dabbler
Active Citizen
Around the Town
Girl Scouting Everywhere
Hands Around the World
Junior Citizen
Local Lore
My Community
Wide World
World Neighbors
Dabbler
Aerospace
Business-Wise
Computer Fun
Do-It-Yourself
Energy Saver
Food, Fibers and Farming
Food Raiser
Science Sleuth
Water Wonders
Dabbler
Architecture
Art in the Home
Art in the Round
Art to Wear
Books
Communication Arts
Dance
Textiles and Fibers
Theatre
Visual Arts
Dabbler
Bicycling
Boating
Eco-Action
Ecology
Finding Your Way
Foot Traveler
Swimming
Troop Camper
Water Fun
Wildlife
Careers
Communication
Healthy Living
Leadership
Looking Your Best
Technology
Your and Your Community
Your Outdoor Surroundings
Wider Opportunities
Folk Arts
Musician
Music Lover
Popular Arts
Prints and Graphics
Individual Sports
Personal Health
Hiker
Horseback Rider
Horse Lover
Outdoor Cook
Outdoor Fun
My Heritage
On My Way
Peoples of the USA
The World in My Community
Traveler
Math Whiz
Ms Fix-It
Putting Things Together
Science Around Town
Science in Action

nesses and the affection shown to me, and to say how greatly I have rejoiced over the way in which you have all carried out your share in the work of the Movement that my beloved husband invented, for the advancement of boys and girls of all countries, years ago. . . . I trust that you will continue fully to use the system of work and play that our Movement provides, keeping up the fun and the friendships made at your meetings and in camps, abiding by the Promise and upholding the Laws that you undertook to live by when you joined up. In that way you will not only advance yourself in body, mind and spirit, but you will affect those around you, in doing what is honorable and right and wise, and in giving out kindness of thought and action, thus striving against all ills and helping to make the world a happier and a better place in which to live.'

From its spontaneous beginnings, Girl Guides evolved into a network of sisterhood that now covers the world. Each of the 108 countries that presently belongs to the World Association of Girl Guides and Girl Scouts has a different woman to thank for bringing the Girl Guide movement to her nation, but it is certain that members the world over celebrate their common history by honoring Agnes, Olave and Lord Baden-Powell, on their special days.

The international sisterhood of Girl Guides and Girl Scouts shares special symbols and customs the world over. The Girl Scout Promise, although spoken in different languages, has a similar meaning in each of the 108 countries where Girl Guides and Girl Scouts are found. Each girl promises to try her best to serve God and her country, to help other people and to live by the Girl Guide or Girl Scout law.

The Girl Scout sign is linked to the Girl Scout Promise. The sign is made with three fingers, which stand for the three parts of the Promise. Using her right hand, a Girl Guide or Girl Scout holds the middle three fingers straight up and holds her littlest finger with her thumb. Whenever the Girl Scout Promise is made, the Sign is also made. The Sign is also appropriate when a girl is invested into a troop, and when she receives a patch or badge. The Sign is the way any Girl Guide or Girl Scout would greet other Girl Guides or Girl Scouts from her troop, a different troop, a different region or from another country. The Sign speaks all languages.

The Girl Scout handshake is another greeting for other Girl Scouts and Girl Guides, although it is more formal. The Girl Scout Handshake is different from a regular handclasp because it is given with the left hand. At the same time the left hand is offered, the right hand is giving the Girl Scout sign.

Another shared signal is the quiet sign, understood by all Girl Guides and Girl Scouts. It is very helpful in large gatherings when many people are speaking at once. The person in charge raises high her right hand. She doesn't need to shout or call for silence. Everyone in the gathering, recognizing the quiet sign, then raises her own right hand and ceases to speak. When everyone has made her own quiet sign, there is quiet.

A friendship circle is sometimes formed in a meeting or around a campfire. Girl Guides and Girl Scouts and their leaders stand in a circle. Each one crosses her right arm over her left and clasps hands with her neighbors. Everyone is silent as a friendship squeeze is started; it is a soft

Above: **These two young ladies posing with their walking sticks are members of the 1st Bollington, Chesire Girl Guides, circa 1910.** *Overleaf:* **At an international encampment, Girl Scouts and Girl Guides from several nations pay rapt attention as an older sister in Girl Scouting/Girl Guiding dons her hat.**

squeeze of the hand from one girl to the girl next to her. The second girl passes the squeeze to the girl next to her, and so on until everyone in the friendship circle has both received and passed on the friendship squeeze. When Girl Guides or Girl Scouts form a friendship circle, they understand that their small circle is a symbol of the unbroken chain of friendship that binds Girl Guides and Girl Scouts all around the world.

The Girl Scout motto in English is 'Be Prepared.' Girls in Spanish-speaking countries say 'Siempre Lista' which means 'always ready.' In Arabic the words are 'Stad-eedoo' which means 'Stand Ready.' In any language the motto means that Girl Guides and Girl Scouts learn how to do things so they will be ready and able to help whenever they are needed.

The Girl Scout slogan is 'Do a Good Turn Daily' which means that each girl will do something to help someone else every day. It also means that a Good Turn does not expect any reward except the good feeling imparted to the girl who offers the Good Turn. The Good Turn can be carried out at the troop level by service projects. At home, the Good Turn might mean putting a bandage on a smaller child's cut. Good Turns do not have to be big projects or take a lot of time. They do not have to be directed toward the same person or done repeatedly. To do a Good Turn daily is to keep the Girl Scout Promise in helping others.

The membership pin of the World Association of Girl Guides and Girl Scouts features a trefoil (like a three-leaved clover), symbolizing the three-part Promise made

Left: **An adult Girl Scout leader strikes a patriot-perfect pose, inspired by her vintage Girl Scout uniform, at a Girl Scout historic uniform pageant.** *Above:* **Leaders of the Botswana Girl Guides (in darker blue dresses) are welcomed to the 25th World Conference at Tarrytown, New York in 1984.**

by each girl. The pin also has two stars which stand for the Promise and the Law. The vein in the middle of the trefoil stands for the compass needle that points the way to go. The base stands for the flames of international friendship, and the blue and gold colors stand for the blue sky and the sun that shines on children all over the world. The World Association flag features the same trefoil and the same colors.

Highlighting the significance of special times and allowing participants to share the moment with others, ceremonies are important to Girl Guide or Girl Scout programs. Ceremonies are intended to be solemn yet celebratory events signifying the development as a good citizen of the country in which they are held. Ceremonies range from local to national and international levels, but each leaves its participants knowledgeable of the special purpose and significance of the ceremony: it celebrates a worldwide sisterhood.

Young members of the Scout movement learn through repeated experiences how to conduct ceremonies and may become proficient in planning and carrying them out to their true purpose. The ceremonies may be varied in location or manner, but Girl Guides and Girl Scouts learn from the tradition to 'look wider still' at the world of possibilities.

The investiture ceremony is for girls who are just joining the organization at any age. The focus is therefore upon the new member herself, as she makes her promise to be true to the ideals of Scouting. The particular words vary from country to country, but in all settings the girl who is being invested learns the meaning of her commit-

ment, to the extent that her age allows her to comprehend.

Investiture is not a public ceremony. It takes place at the troop level, and people special to the participants may be invited—such as parents and family members. Because it is a time of celebration and well-wishing, a party may follow the ceremony.

Rededication is called by various names throughout the world, and may take place at the same time as investiture. Girls who are already members of Girl Guides or Girl Scouts reaffirm themselves to the ideals of the Scouting movement.

Receiving the specific headwear of a unit (determined by age) is called a capping ceremony. The headwear may be presented by senior members of the group or by adult advisors. The significance of the ceremony embodies readiness to meet challenges ahead as young women.

The flag ceremony demonstrates reverence and respect for the flag of one's country. Flag etiquette is part of all Girl Guide and Girl Scout programs, and the presence of a national flag along with the organization's flag symbolizes the respect that Girl Guides and Girl Scouts all over the world hold for good citizenship and service. Membership in a color guard—a group that carries the flags—is an honor and a responsibility.

Lord Baden-Powell described the Scouts' Own ceremony's 'voluntary uplifting of hearts . . . in thanksgiving for the joys of life' as 'quiet and reverent moments of communion together.'

A Scouts' Own ceremony may be either elaborately planned or spontaneous. Any time that Scouts or Guides are gathered together is an appropriate time. Themes for a Scouts' Own may be the beauty of the outdoors or honor or courage or kindness or music—any of these themes

Upper left: Girl Scouts and Girl Guides from all over the world gathered at the opening ceremonies for the 15th World Conference at Tarrytown, New York. *Lower left:* These Girl Scouts listen attentively as the Air Force instructor teaches them first aid. *Above:* These Girl Guides practiced first aid in 1910. *At right:* The Hove Girl Guides of Sussex are shown bringing books to a Red Cross library in 1919.

among many others is suitable for the 'uplifting of hearts.' A Scouts' Own ceremony with a nature theme might be held outdoors, perhaps in the forest. One of the Scouts might read an inspirational poem about the beauty of nature before a time of silent reflection. Some of the Scouts or Guides might want to share their thoughts with the group. Perhaps the ceremony would conclude with a song.

Since no pattern exists for a Scouts' Own, any part of this example might be eliminated or expanded. A Scouts' Own with a nature theme could be celebrated in complete silence or wholly in music.

The ceremonies that bestow the insignia of the association may be incorporated into other ceremonies. The presentation of the World Association pin, for instance, usually coincides with investiture.

An excerpt from the February 1927 *Girl Guide Gazette* written by Rose Kerr neatly summarizes the idea behind 'Thinking Day:'

'At the World Conference in the United States of America [1926] it was suggested by one of the French delegates that there should be an international 'Thinking Day' on which the Guides of all our different countries should remember each other, and send messages of friendship and goodwill flashing across the world by the wireless of thought. The proposal was adopted with acclamation, but it was not so easy to select a day. The one which was

Above: These Brownies, photographed in 1918 while doing their exercises, hailed from Weston-super-Mare, an English borough on the Bristol channel. During the World War I years, Girl Guides proved themselves by doing service work of all kinds, including driving ambulances. In photos circa 1914-18, Guides (*left*) help a sick man into his wheelchair at a military hospital, and (*right*) clean windows and shine shoes. These contemporary Scouts (*overleaf*) learn about past cultures.

finally chosen is February 22nd, which is a great day for us because it is the birthday of the Chief Scout [Robert Baden-Powell], and also by an extraordinary coincidence, of the Chief Guide [Olave Baden-Powell].'

Sixty years later Thinking Day is still celebrated all over the world. It remains a time for girls to consider the international dimensions of their movement, which is now over eight million members strong.

No set pattern for Thinking Day celebrations exists, and local traditions have developed for its various celebrations, such as parties with an international theme, gathering to watch the sunrise or worshipping with others if the troop shares a religion. However it is celebrated, the emphasis is on thinking of others.

Graduation marks not the end of service and achievements by members of Girl Guides and Girl Scouts, but the beginning of adulthood. A graduate may wish to speak about the principles of Scouting and what the Promise and Law have meant to her. Also, usually each girl's achievements as a Scout or Guide are highlighted in the ceremony.

A farewell party for graduates may follow the graduation

ceremony, for the event is meant to be a joyful passage dramatizing the meaning of Scouting throughout life.

THE WORLD CENTERS

Girl Guides and Girl Scouts from the whole world meet at the four world centers: Olave House, Our Cabaña, Our Chalet, and Sangam. The centers are owned and operated by the World Association of Girl Guides and Girl Scouts (WAGGGS), and the world flag is flown at each center. The world trefoil is displayed prominently at each center—on the dinner plates at Our Chalet, on the front gate at Sangam, and on the entrance door to Our Cabaña.

Girl Guides and Girl Scouts of any age may visit the centers during the day. Senior Girl Scouts and adults may, as individuals or troops, make reservations (well in advance!) to stay at a center for several days.

Olave House has not always been the name of the world center in London. The original world center in England was a five-story town house called Our Ark. It was opened in London in 1939. During World War II, Our Ark housed many Girl Guides who had to leave their homes because of the war. When peace arrived, even more Girl Guide and Girl Scout travelers arrived at Our Ark. Soon two London townhouses, joined by passageways on the top and bottom floors, housed all the travelers. In 1963 the name of Our Ark was changed to Olave House, in honor of Lady Olave Baden-Powell.

Anyone who has ever been a Girl Guide or Girl Scout may stay here while she visits the sights of London. Visitors often enjoy late afternoon tea in Olave House's lovely walled garden while sharing travel and Scouting experiences.

On the bulletin board in the entryway of Olave House is mounted a large map of London, to help visitors situate

At left: **Composed of two connected town houses, Our Ark—the World Center in London—was renamed Olave House in honor of Lady Baden-Powell.** *Above:* **The Our Cabaña World Center opened in 1957 and is located in Cuernavaca, Mexico.**

themselves. Places of interest, as well as hospitals, banks and post offices are all marked on the map with directions to these places posted nearby.

Olave House is open all year as a hostel except for occasional WAGGGS seminars or World Committee meetings. Olave House does not have the varied programs that the other world centers do, but it holds a special place of admiration for Girl Guides and Girl Scouts from all over because of its historic importance, and location: London, after all, was where Lord Baden-Powell started Boy Scouting and Girl Guiding.

Our Cabaña is the 'Spanglish' name for the world center located in Mexico. In Spanish this beautiful stone-walled retreat is called 'Nuestra Cabaña.' Opened in 1957 and located in Cuernavaca, Mexico the architectural style of Our Cabaña reflects the Spanish influence that permeates the rest of the town. Tropical flowers and vines cover the outside walls which enclose several low buildings—the dining room, crafts center and dormitories. Our Cabaña literally blooms year-round in Cuernavaca's tropical climate. Each year, near the last week of February, a big jacaranda tree nearly explodes with white blossoms! Since the blossoms seem to add to the Thinking Day celebration of Lord and Lady Baden-Powell's mutual birthday (February 22), Our Cabaña's jacaranda is called the 'Thinking Day Tree.'

From Our Cabaña visitors can see the dormant volcanoes *Popocateptl* and *Iztaccihuatl* in the distance. Also available to visitors is a chance to enjoy the beautiful surrounding areas of Mexico. Taxco, a tiny hillside town known for its silver mines, is not too far from Our Cabaña by car, and many Girl Guide or Girl Scout visitors have returned to their homes with souvenirs of *plata de Taxco*, silver from Taxco. Also accessible, but about twice as far

Scouts and Guides enjoy outdoor activities of all kinds at Our Chalet *(above)* **in Switzerland—including tree planting** *(right).*

as Taxco, is Mexico City, the busy capital of Mexico. Cuernavaca itself contains a number of scenic interests including Cortez's palace, a colonial cathedral and a colorful marketplace.

However, it is not for the other sights that visitors come to Our Cabaña. They come to enjoy the arts and music of Mexico, which are a specialty of Our Cabaña. The crafts center is full of supplies to be used to make *piñatas, corazones de trigo* (straw figures), bark paintings, ceramics and *nearikas* (yarn paintings). Nearly every Cabaña session includes the arts, and the sessions for girls or adults devoted to folk arts and music are particularly popular.

Sharing equal importance with the arts at Our Cabaña is the Community Recreation Project in the parish of Gualupita. Hundreds of local children have participated in this recreation project, which attracts Girl Guides and Girl Scouts from all over the world who exchange crafts and games with the children in Mexico.

Part of each session at Our Cabaña includes a program on the problem of world hunger where participants are helped to understand this global issue. Great pains are taken to prevent wasted food at Our Cabaña. In the midst of the beauty that surrounds them, participants at Our Cabaña remember the elements of the Girl Scout Law that encourage them to be helpful and responsible citizens.

Our Chalet was a gift of Mrs. Helen Osborne Storrow (a friend of Girl Scouting in the United States), and was opened as a world center in 1932. It is located on the side of an Alpine mountain not too far from the village of Adelboden in Switzerland. Its location is perfect for many outdoor activities throughout the year.

In the summer, visitors can explore the beautiful landscape on foot, walking down to the lumber mill and then following the path along a stream up to the waterfall. Alpine meadows thick with flowers make a nice stop along the way. A chair lift to the top of the mountain allows a magnificent view of Our Chalet, tiny far below. Photographs of the breathtaking views and images of new and old friends find their way home with all the visitors of Our Chalet.

Winter activities include tobogganing, cross-country skiing and downhill skiing with instruction from Our Chalet staff. Our Chalet's big open fireplace welcomes tired visitors home in the evening when folk dancing, singing in many languages and other indoor activities come alive.

Guests at Our Chalet who have come for special Girl Guide and Girl Scout sessions eat and sleep there. They also help take care of it. Others, who do not plan to attend sessions but just want to camp for one or two nights, may stay in Squirrel House (a cabin with a hayloft for sleeping quarters) or at the camp site near Our Chalet.

Sangam opened in 1966. Located in the hills southeast of Bombay, India, Sangam is on the outskirts of the town of Poona. In Sanskrit 'Sangam' means 'coming together,' as in the way small rivers flow into one main stream; at Sangam girls and adults come together from India, other parts of Asia and other countries for a variety of events.

Girls and adults have the chance to participate in community service projects in Poona and other nearby villages, or to volunteer as staff for an occasional resident camp session for local girls. Some events at Sangam feature Indian music and dance, arts and crafts or religion. Training sessions for adults from nearby countries are

held at Sangam, and sometimes Girl Guides and Girl Scouts meet there to discuss issues.

Mild and warm weather the year round encourages the center's flowering trees, vegetable garden and formal flower beds. Girls may work in Sangam's vegetable garden or help harvest bananas and sugarcane. They also may work in the peanut garden, which was started with the help of a Girl Scout council from the United States after a session at Sangam on world hunger.

Across the road from Sangam is the Phulenagar Colony, a housing development for low income people. Visiting Girl Guides and Girl Scouts may help Phulenagar Colony families with sewing, cooking, hygiene and nutrition. They also plan classes and activities for the children.

THE THINKING DAY FUND

At the 1932 (seventh) World Conference held in Poland, a Belgian Girl Guide leader proposed that each Girl Guide or Girl Scout be asked to give a penny, or whatever was appropriate in her own currency, to a Thinking Day Fund. The Fund would be used to put into practice the principles of international sisterhood, which formed the basis of Thinking Day. The original 'Thinking Day Penny' is now symbolic and Girl Guides and Girl

Scouts give whatever they can afford.

The Thinking Day Fund helps to bring the Scouting movement to girls in all parts of the world by providing expert help to members and prospective members in organizing an active Girl Guide or Girl Scout association to develop a program suited to their own needs and resources. It promotes friendship between girls of all nationalities, races and religions through international camps, conferences and World Center sessions. The Fund makes it possible for leaders to partake of training in countries other than their own. The Fund sends relief to Girl Guides and Girl Scouts suffering from such natural and manmade disasters as floods, famines and wars in any of the countries whose national organizations are members of the World Association of Girl Guides and Girl Scouts (WAGGGS). The Fund cooperates with other international voluntary agencies with similar aims.

Contributions to the Thinking Day Fund are collected by the national organizations and forwarded for international administration.

Above: **The Sangam World Center is located near Poona, India, not far from Bombay. Activities for visiting Scouts include gardening, classes in Indian culture and religion, and helping out with needed domestic skills at the nearby Phulenagar Colony low-income housing project. World Centers help Scouts and Guides to reach a deeper sense of world wide sisterhood, and to broaden their skills. *At right* are members of the Thailand Girl Scout/Girl Guide movement.**

GIRL SCOUTING IN THE UNITED STATES

Girl Scouts of the USA is the largest voluntary organization for girls in the world. Nearly 2.3 million girls and over a half million adults belong to this organization for girls that teaches them to contribute to society and encourages them to develop their own interests and abilities. The Girl Scout program of work, play and companionship is open to all girls from age five to seventeen (or in kindergarten through grade 12) who subscribe to Girl Scout ideals. Girl Scouts of the USA is a member of the World Association of Girl Guides and Girl Scouts which embraces 108 countries in its worldwide family. Its program is an adventure in learning that offers girls a broad range of activities which address both their current interests and their future roles as women.

Girl Scouts make the Girl Scout Promise:
>   On my honor, I will try:
>   To serve God and my country,
>   To help people at all times
>   And to live by the Girl Scout Law.
and try to follow the Girl Scout Law:
>   I will do my best:
>   To be honest
>   To be fair
>   To help where I am needed
>   To be cheerful
>   To be friendly and considerate
>   To be a sister to every Girl Scout
>   To respect authority
>   To use resources wisely
>   To protect and improve the world around me
>   To show respect for myself and others through my
>   words and actions.

The Girl Scout (and Girl Guide) emblem is a trefoil, like a three-leaf clover, which represents the three parts of the Girl Scout Promise. The symbol of Girl Scouts of the USA has three young women's profiles on the trefoil's face.

Left: **American Girl Scouts gather under a magnificent rock formation—one of the attractions of the Girl Scout National Center West at Tensleep, Wyoming.** *Upper Right:* **These are pins signifying membership in the contemporary Girl Scouts of the USA, including at** *upper left,* **a Brownie Girl Scout pin. Note the stylish sophisticated look of the lower two pins.**

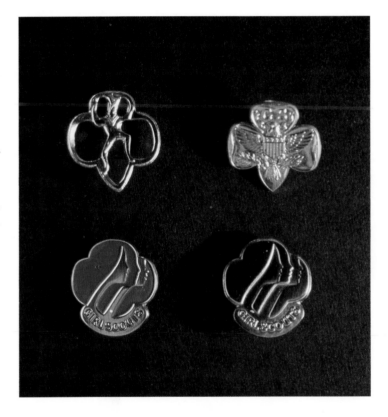

The Girl Scout program has five levels: Daisy Girl Scouts, Brownie Girl Scouts, Junior Girl Scouts, Cadette Girl Scouts and Senior Girl Scouts. A girl may enter at any level appropriate to her age whether or not she already has experience in Girl Scouting. For instance, a girl may join at the Cadette level even if she has not been a Junior, Brownie or Daisy Girl Scout.

The national headquarters in New York City carries out the goals and policies of the organization, a non-profit corporation.

Juliette Gordon Low founded the Girl Scouts of the United States of America when she organized the first Girl Scout Troop in Savannah, Georgia on 12 March 1912. With the words 'I've got something for the girls of Savannah and all America and all the world, and we're going to start it tonight,' Juliette Low began a program that gave girls a chance to develop their potential.

Juliette had been born in Savannah, Georgia on 31 October 1860, just a few months before the Civil War.

Above: London Girl Guides learn firefighting in 1940. *At right:* Girl Scouts USA was born here in 1912—in Savannah, at what is now the Juliette Gordon Low National Center—as the American Girl Guides, renamed the 'Girl Scouts' in 1913.

Because her mother was from the North and her father from the South, Juliette's first years were spent both in Savannah and in Chicago, her mother's home. She was four and a half years old by the time the Civil War ended.

Juliette grew up with the nickname 'Daisy,' given to her by one of her uncles when she was born. He had taken one look at her and declared, 'I bet she's going to be a daisy!' The name was appropriate for the girl who made up her own games, wrote and performed her own plays and started a magazine when she was still a child. Daisy's magazine lasted five years; it featured only children as authors and illustrators. Each contributor took as a pen name the name of a flower. Daisy already had her name.

Daisy loved to form clubs. One story in the present-day Brownie handbook tells of a club Daisy formed called 'Helping Hands' for which Daisy had decided to be the sewing teacher. A complicating circumstance was that Daisy did not know how to sew, and the club members were nicknamed the 'helpless hands' before they were able to carry out their sewing service projects.

When she was a teenager Daisy suffered an ear infection which left her partially deaf in one ear. Then, on her wedding day, a celebrating guest threw some rice for good luck which went into her other ear. A doctor tried to remove the rice, but the result was that Daisy totally lost her hearing in that ear.

Not stopped by her handicap, Juliette Gordon Low continued to be an active, popular and friendly person. Daisy Low was living in Scotland when she heard about the Scouting movement for girls. In 1911 when she was travelling in England, she met Lord Baden-Powell, the founder of Boy Scouting, at a luncheon. She became so enthused that she began a Scottish Girl Guide troop. The troop met at her home on Saturday afternoons, and some of the seven girls walked as far as six miles to attend. Daisy used as her manual *How Girls Can Help to Build Up the Empire*, published by Lord Baden-Powell's sister Agnes. Following the manual, her troop learned knots, flag history, Girl Guide laws, knitting, cooking, first aid, map reading and signaling. Daisy also tried to prepare the girls to earn a living by helping them learn such useful skills as raising chickens and spinning. She started other Girl Guide troops in London before she returned to America to begin the first American troop, in Savannah.

Daisy's cousin, Nina Pape, shared Daisy's enthusiasm for the Girl Guides after she heard how much the girls learned both indoor and out-of-doors. Nina was a teacher who thought that some of the girls at her school would be interested in Scouting. They were. Eighteen girls met at Daisy's house for their first meeting in 1912.

The Savannah girls copied the uniforms of the British Girl Guides: long skirts and blouses of dark blue with light blue ties. They had no patterns, but sewed them themselves and also made their badges by hand.

Other troops sprang up in Savannah and in other parts of the United States. The Savannah troops enjoyed an inter-troop basketball league on a court set up across from Daisy's house. They all learned the Girl Guide law, played games, went on nature hikes and kept bird books from their bird watching.

Some of Daisy's troop were among the fifty or so girls at Georgia's Camp Lowlands, the first Girl Scout camp, held in the summer of 1912. Photographs of the group at Camp Lowlands show a group of smiling young girls standing proud in their handmade uniforms, the first of their kind in the United States.

Left: **Here, at the 43rd national convention, former national president Jane Freeman encourages two Daisies to step forward in proclaiming the introduction of the Daisy level of Scouting.** *Above:* **A Daisy solemnly gives the Scout sign.**

The name of the American Girl Guides was changed to the Girl Scouts in 1913, and the girls decided to change the color of their uniforms from blue to khaki because khaki was more practical—it didn't show the dirt as much.

That same year Daisy set up a national organization with headquarters in Washington, DC. The Girl Scouts of the USA was incorporated in Washington, DC on 10 June 1915. It was chartered by the US Congress on 16 March 1950.

Juliette Gordon Low died in 1927; she had made good her promise to the girls of the United States. On that night in 1912 she surely had 'something for the girls'— something that has enriched the lives of over 49 million girls since then. While specific activities have changed over the years to keep pace with the changing interests of girls, the original commitment to fully developing the potential of each member has not.

Girl Scouting helps today's girls become productive, self-confident, socially responsible women. GSUSA works toward that goal by reflecting the contemporary world in its informal education program. Highlighting four areas of contemporary concern—non-stereotyped career education, the sciences, sports for women, and leadership development—GSUSA has much to offer every American girl.

Career exploration programs exist at all age levels of Girl Scouting. Non-sexist, non-racist and non-sectarian material provides career education intended to help girls determine career goals without restrictions. Guiding girls in career choices is a contemporary challenge facing GSUSA.

The ever-increasing role of science in daily life has been recognized by GSUSA. The organization has taken steps to familiarize its members with scientific development and technologies.

GSUSA actively promotes the participation of women and girls in team and individual sports, recognizing that a healthy body and an educated mind work together to create productive citizens.

GSUSA tries to prepare girls for leadership roles by helping them explore options and to take active roles in determining their futures.

Contemporary concern areas are reflected in the total Girl Scout program—evident in their handbooks and other publications, their awards, their uniforms and their equipment.

Adult volunteers, both women and men, number approximately 624,000. Volunteer work is an opportunity for personal growth—the opportunity to interact with young people, or the chance to work in a husband-wife team, or work out a personal challenge. The experience of volunteer work provides an environment rich in human contacts that allows the volunteer a chance to learn more about herself or himself while contributing to society. Adult volunteers usually involve themselves in Girl Scouting as troop leaders.

Although they receive no monetary rewards for their contributions to Girl Scouting, adult volunteers benefit from the leadership and management skills they develop

in their roles. These transferable skills can be a benefit to adult volunteers who have not yet established themselves in a career, using their experience with Girl Scouting and those same skills to later secure paid positions. Continuing Education Units (CEUs) are available for workshops and seminars sponsored for adults by GSUSA.

The Edith Macy Conference Center located in Briarcliff Manor, New York provides a modern training environment for volunteer and paid staff. This national training and conference complex reflects GSUSA's commitment to developing skills for its staff. The Edith Macy Center enjoys easy access to New York City and is available for use by non-Girl Scout groups.

Girl Scouting has always encouraged its members to look beyond themselves to the larger community. Even local experiences, such as field trips, broaden a member's view of the world and help that member to discover her place in it. The creator of Scouting, Lord Baden-Powell, encouraged his first troops to 'Look wide! And when you think you are looking wide, look wider still.' Girl Scouts USA enthusiastically follows his advice.

In its general membership, adult volunteers, paid staff and national board of directors, GSUSA is a multiracial, multicultural organization with significant participation by minority groups. Girl Scout Handbooks are published not only in English, but also in Spanish and in Braille.

Firsthand opportunities to expand horizons are provided to Girl Scouts and adult members by their local councils and the national organization. Called 'wider opportunities,' these events often involve travel to one of GSUSA's national centers: the Juliette Gordon Low home in Savannah Georgia; Girl Scout National Center West, the 14,000-acre Wyoming wilderness retreat; and the Edith Macy Conference Center near New York City.

There are even American Girl Scout troops in other countries. Troops on foreign soil (TOFS) was created by GSUSA in 1927 to extend the benefits of Girl Scouting to American girls living with their families overseas. Now called USA Girl Scouts Overseas, its membership numbers over 21,000 and includes a diversity of areas, from the United Kingdom to islands in the South Pacific.

Girl Scouts USA is an active member of the World Association of Girl Guides and Girl Scouts (WAGGGS), the organization formed to promote unity of purpose and common understanding of the principles of Girl Scouting throughout the world. WAGGGS maintains the four world centers, and it encourages Girl Scouts and Girl Guides the world over to visit them.

GSUSA is recognized as a non-governmental organization affiliated with the Department of Public Information at the United Nations. The World Association holds consultative status with several United Nations committees and, as such, often provides background information and commentary to those committees regarding international issues affecting women and girls.

The goals of the Girl Scout program are stated in its four program emphases: developing self potential, relating to others, developing values and contributing to society. These goals are the consistent aims of the program— no matter the age of the individual Girl Scouts.

Left: **Girl Scouts board member Ruth Framk enjoys a meeting with Jim Fowler, host of the Mutual of Omaha television show** *Wild Kingdom,* **at the 25th World Conference in 1984.** *Overleaf:* **These Scouts exploring the World of Art study a sculpture.**

Within the first emphasis, developing self potential, the Girl Scout program works to foster feelings of self-acceptance and individual self-worth in each Scout. Each girl is encouraged to see herself as competent, responsible and open to new experiences and challenges. She is encouraged in her personal growth.

The second emphasis, relating to others, aims to help girls interact with other people with increasing understanding, skill and respect. To achieve this relationship, each girl is encouraged to develop sensitivity to others by respecting the needs, feelings and rights of others. The Girl Scout program promotes understanding and appreciation of individual cultural, religious and racial differences by including all girls, regardless of background. In this way the program promotes the ability in girls to build friendships and working relationships with people who may be different from themselves.

The third emphasis, developing values, seeks to provide a foundation for sound decision-making. The program helps each Girl Scout to develop a meaningful set of values and ethics that will guide her actions. It fosters her ability to make decisions that are consistent with her values and that reflect respect for the rights and needs of others. The program further encourages her to reexamine her ideals as she grows and changes.

The fourth emphasis of the Girl Scout program, contributing to society, aims to improve society by teaching a girl to use her abilities and leadership skills to cooperatively work with others in the world at large. The program develops concern for the well-being of the Girl

Scout's community and its people. It promotes an understanding of how the quality of community life affects each Girl Scout and all of society, and encourages her ultimately to use her skills to work with others for the benefit of all.

The Girl Scout program is divided to meet the developmental, educational, emotional and social needs and interests of girls at five age levels. The emphases of the Daisy Girl Scout program are the same as those of the Senior Girl Scout program. Their particular activities, however, may be different because a 17-year-old Girl Scout contributes to society differently than a 5-year-old— a high-school Scout has a different perception of her abilities than a kindergartner. Each one nevertheless ascribes to her Girl Scout Promise and the Girl Scout Law, and contributes what she is able as she continues to develop.

The four program emphases are supported by a troop atmosphere of openness, freedom and trust that encourages each girl's growth. Each girl in the Girl Scout program is encouraged to discover ways to express herself and communicate with others, in order to understand and appreciate other people and other cultures. She is encouraged to make choices from among real alternatives, to grapple with and solve problems. Recognizing her own talents and building on them, she can take responsibility for her actions, use her own knowledge and skills in challenging situations, and help develop standards for her own behavior and accomplishment. She can make mistakes without the stigma of failure. She can have fun, build friendships and become an active part of her com-

munity. She is encouraged to explore many roles and to discover the unlimited potential of becoming a woman.

The Girl Scout program is for *all* girls. At each age level the program encourages pluralism as it promotes racial and ethnic pride and respect. In each of its activities and experiences, the program encourages leadership development and decision-making skills through self-government, partnerships with adults and the influence of adult role models. It promotes cooperative learning experience in group dynamics under the guidance of trained adults, and builds skills through progressive experiences for each Girl Scout at every age level.

Service is an important element of the Girl Scout program which encourages girls to develop into responsible citizens. Understanding and performing services to the group (her family, her troop, her religious group, her community) lays the foundation for a Girl Scout's responsibility for her future actions as a woman.

Girl Scouts of the USA is a non-profit corporation financed chiefly by Girl Scout membership dues which provide approximately 40 percent of total revenues. The sale of uniforms and equipment provides another 37 percent. The remainder of the Girl Scouts of the USA budget comes from investments, gifts and miscellaneous sources.

Local councils generate the bulk of their revenue from product sales which include the famous Girl Scout cookies and Girl Scout calendars; 47 percent of an average council's budget comes from product sales. About 25 percent of a council's budget is provided by United Way funds. Other council revenues come from investments,

The World Association of Girl Guides and Girl Scouts promotes international education and friendship.

Left: Ronald Reagan, also a Boy Scout supporter, tells these Scouts to 'keep up the good work.' *Above:* An international Scouting exhibit. *Below:* These two Circle T Council Scouts explore broadcasting as a possible career choice.

fund development efforts and miscellaneous sources. While the United Way contributes importantly to local Girl Scout councils, the national Girl Scout organization receives no funding from the United Way.

All the proceeds from the sale of Girl Scout cookies remain with the local council in which the cookies were sold, and individual troops retain a portion of their own cookie sales. In addition to providing revenue for the Girl Scout program, cookie sales teach girls skills in salesmanship, marketing and money management. Because cookies are often pre-ordered (girls take orders before the cookies are delivered), the follow-through actions of making deliveries and collecting money for each box of cookies often leans responsibility onto very young shoulders. In some councils, direct sales take place—usually via 'cookie booths' in shopping malls, banks or other high-traffic areas. Sharing the financial responsibility for their own activities is one way in which girls may discern—and progress—from dreams to reality.

Above: A Girl Scout color guard. *At right*—Scouting in the 1950s. Brownie Nadine Zolokovich and Scout Maria Tariggino present Dr Herbert Clish with a Girl Scout Calendar (*top*). Secretary of the Army Wilbur Brucker buys cookies from Scout Mary Coughlin and her sister, Brownie Pat Coughlin (*bottom*).

As part of its corporate planning process, Girl Scouts USA establishes corporate goals adopted by its National Board of Directors which provide direction for the total organization. Helping to shape the corporate goals for 1985 to 1990 were National Board committees, national staff, and Girl Scout councils. Girl Scouts USA's most recent corporate goals include all phases of the Girl Scout organization:

Girl Scouts USA will try to attract more members and to develop a diverse leadership, and will plan ways to help girls develop decision-making abilities. The program will help girls first understand and then take action on personal, community and global issues that affect their present and future well-being. Girl Scouts USA will elimi-

Above: **US National Girl Scout President Mrs Betty F Pillsbury** (*center*) **chairs a leadership panel.** *Right:* **These Brownies mount a sales campaign for Girl Scout cookies.** *Overleaf:* **Daisies and their leaders in the World of the Out-of-Doors.**

nate institutional racism throughout the Girl Scout movement and will seek to gather members from as many ethnic groups as possible. The organization will discuss the needs of girls and women to make sure that Girl Scouting continues to contribute to a changing society.

A wider diversity of funding sources will finance the organization. The organization will emphasize adult responsibility for financing the total Girl Scout organization, rather than youth members' responsibility, and will ensure that structures, relationships and decision-making systems are flexible, productive and responsive to the needs of members, councils and the community.

These corporate goals speak eloquently for the aims of the national Girl Scout organization—to build on the foundation laid by Juliette Low, whose expressed goal was to meet the needs of American girls. Since its beginnings, Girl Scouts of the USA has believed that young girls deserve broader opportunities for expanding their horizons. GSUSA remains in the vanguard, anticipating the needs of girls and designing innovative program ideas to answer those needs.

The desire to maintain a contemporary and attractive image is evident in the many changes of uniform styles chosen by Girl Scouts USA. The very first uniforms were homesewn, but in 1916, official uniforms became available from the national organization. Leading clothing designers have created the more modern uniforms, beginning in 1948 when Mainbocher designed new uniforms for all age levels. In 1978 Halston designed a five-part adult uniform, and in 1984 Bill Blass designed a seven-piece adult uniform plus accessories. Comfort and contemporary good looks have always been the challenge to uniform designers.

DAISY GIRL SCOUTS

A girl who is five to six years old (or in kindergarten through first grade) may become a Daisy Girl Scout by attending troop meetings and learning the Girl Scout Promise and the Girl Scout Law. At a special ceremony called investiture she receives a Daisy Girl Scout pin and a certificate. She may wear an official Daisy uniform—a blue tunic that ties over her regular clothing, somewhat like a pinafore.

Daisies have the opportunity to learn about and believe in themselves through small-group involvement. They develop an understanding of good citizenship and an awareness of the world through activities that are fun.

An adult volunteer, sometimes aided by an older Girl Scout, leads the troop. The leader tries to give each child the opportunity to develop a positive self-image, gain knowledge of her world and how it functions, share in making the decisions that affect her life, share her ideas with others, play and re-create her experiences, and to grow socially and develop self control.

IT'S GIRL SCOUT COOKIE TIME

Daisy Girl Scouts are named after 'Daisy' Gordon Low, whose real name was Juliette Gordon Low, the founder of Girl Scouts of the USA. All Girl Scouts of the United States honor 'Daisy' Low on her birthday, and Daisy Girl Scouts strive to honor their namesake by being good Girl Scouts.

Daisy Girl Scouts enjoy activities from all five 'worlds of interest' used throughout the Girl Scouts of the United States program. Daisy Girl Scout activities reflect the interests of each troop, and are geared to the age level of Daisy Girl Scouts, so the activities and projects can be completed successfully and enjoyably.

Activities and games about nutrition, health, safety and physical fitness combine into the World of Well-Being Interest for Daisy Girl Scouts. Learning in this world helps prepare Daisies for working and playing safely.

Daisy visits to firehouses, police stations or health care facilities help them visualize the many people and services that keep their community operating. Within the troop, Daisy Girl Scouts might act out roles of various community helpers or enjoy a visit from one of the helpers—such as a mail carrier or telephone repair person.

Also fun are cooking (and tasting!) activities. The food may be familiar or exotic, and Daisy Girl Scouts can voice their opinions about which foods taste good.

Daisy Girl Scouts are encouraged to begin lifelong good health habits. Reinforcing daily grooming habits is fun when you sing about them. A visit from a health care professional can not only be informative, but also the beginning of career awareness.

Running games like 'Catch the Puppy's Tail' can be part of the World of Well-Being. Many Daisy Girl Scout troops have enjoyed forming the 'Knee Sit-Upon Circle'—a clever way to rest upon each other's knees without the support of furniture.

Other well-being activities center upon home life. 'Family' puppets is one activity that Daisy Girl Scouts can enjoy whatever size or form their families may be. A natural follow-up to this activity is another one—putting on a puppet play.

Whatever World of Well-Being activities the Daisy Girl Scout troop leader plans for her troop, Daisy Girl Scouts in that troop can have fun and learn at the same time.

Through activities in the World of People, Daisy Girl Scouts explore other cultures. Knowledge of similarities and respect for diversity is an important part of Girl Scouting. Daisies begin to learn that while many values are universal, different racial, religious and cultural groups value different things.

Left: These Daisy Girl Scouts demonstrate honoring one's country in a flag ceremony. *Above:* Today, my hand; tomorrow a masterpiece! Receptivity, however, is the key to the World of Art. *Right:* Daisy Girl Scouts take part in a recycling drive.

Celebrations and holidays from many countries can be celebrated. Daisy Girl Scout troops that know the background of a celebration have no trouble joining into a festive occasion. The luckiest Daisy Girl Scout troops are those with members representing many different cultures and religions, since they have the opportunity to learn first-hand from members of their own troop. Although special days are not necessarily festive, learning about them is an excellent opportunity for cultural sharing.

Of course, all activities and opportunities for learning are prepared with the age of the Daisy Girl Scout troop in mind. Therefore Daisy Girl Scouts might celebrate their own birthdays in the manner of another country, learn about Mexican Independence Day by eating bunuelos (sweet cinnamon crisps) or commemorate African Kwanza (harvest festival) with a potluck.

Daisy Girl Scouts love to play games, and international games form a popular part of their World of People interest. The World Association of Girl Guides and Girl Scouts has published a book called *World Games and Recipes*, a

Upper left: **A 'Daisy ring.'** *Lower left:* **These Daisies explore another culture in the World of People with this Mexican piñata.** *Above:* **This Brownie and this Daisy are 'bridging' together. Each is passing to her next Scouting level.**

wonderful resource for Daisy Girl Scout troop leaders. From playing 'Crocodile, May I Cross the River?' to 'El Gato y el Raton,' Daisies take the first steps toward international friendship.

Opportunities for discovery unfold in the World of Today and Tomorrow. With the guidance of the troop leader, through the use of her own talents and in cooperative effort with others, even a Daisy Girl Scout can contribute to the betterment of society. Daisy Girl Scouts can plant flowers for their school, tidy up the ground around their meeting place, or water plants for their families or neighbors. They can compare fingerprints, observe objects through magnifying glasses, make crystal gardens or sprout seeds. Troop leaders try to provide Daisies with opportunities for discovery while letting the girls seek answers for themselves. Field trips to the airport, a farmyard or to city hall are exciting possibilities for discovery. Troop leaders become accustomed to exclamations of 'Look at this!' when their troops experience the World of today and Tomorrow.

Opportunities for expression through various art forms, and appreciation of other people's talents inspire Daisy Girl Scouts in the World of the Arts.

Daisy Girl Scouts learn that ideas and materials for art projects can be found everywhere and sometimes in surprising forms. Simple handclapping is one basis for music. The weather can inspire a drawing or a dance. Simply listening to a good storyteller develops love of language and may inspire creative writing in later years.

Daisy Girl Scout troops love make-believe—a natural beginning for a pantomime or creative interpretation. Painting, sculpture, drawing or stitchery, in varying stages of refinement, are popular activities in the World of

the Arts interest. Some Daisy Girl Scouts might enjoy quiet expressions such as making a collection of dried flowers, while others might create a rhythmic orchestra. Whatever form their expressions take, Daisy Girl Scouts are encouraged to develop their creativity and to use resources wisely.

Camping activities are usually minimal at the Daisy Girl Scout level, but that doesn't mean Daisy Girl Scouts don't enjoy the World of the Out-of-Doors. An enjoyable walk outside with their troop and an attentive adult can be a learning experience. In sharing observations, discoveries and feelings about the experience, Daisy Girl Scouts can begin to grasp the meaning of part of the Girl Scout Law: 'to protect and improve the world around me.'

Daisy Girl Scout troops may hold an occasional outdoor meeting in a park, the schoolyard or someone's backyard, where running and exploring are most inviting. The opportunities and inspirations for out-of-doors activities depend largely upon the geographic setting of each troop. Some troops might take a walk in the snow, some might spend time at the waterfront and some might walk through the cotton fields. No matter the setting, the challenges to the senses and the variety of inspirations from the out-of-doors help Daisies to enjoy exploring their natural environments.

A related activity that Daisy Girl Scouts enjoy is mapping. Girls may construct large three-dimensional maps of their communities and thereby come to understand their environment in a concrete way. As are most Daisy activities, this one is creative, educational and fun all at the same time.

BROWNIE GIRL SCOUTS

Girls from age six to eight (or in grades 1, 2 or 3) can become Brownie Girl Scouts. If a girl has been a Daisy Girl Scout, she participates in a bridging ceremony that symbolizes her progression from Daisy Girl Scout to Brownie Girl Scout. The 'bridge' in the ceremony may be a plank of wood upon which she walks. Awaiting her at the end of the bridge are girls who are already Brownie Girl Scouts and ready to welcome her into their troop. After she crosses the bridge, she receives a Brownie Girl Scout pin and a certificate marking the completion of her year as a Daisy Girl Scout.

If the girl has not previously been a Daisy Girl Scout, she may still become a Brownie Girl Scout if she makes the Girl Scout Promise. She receives a Brownie Girl Scout pin, at an investiture ceremony to which parents or other guests may have been invited. Troops sometimes celebrate an investiture by singing the 'Brownie Smile Song.' The song, found in the Brownie Girl Scout handbook, is soon learned by heart.

Wearing a Brownie Girl Scout uniform is one of the privileges of being a Brownie Girl Scout, although it is not required. If the official uniform should change style while a girl is a Brownie Girl Scout, she may wear the same uniform she already has. The Brownie Girl Scout pin and World Association pin can be worn on regular clothing.

Brownie Girl Scouts practice service at home and in their communities. They work to earn embroidered patch-

Above: **This Daisy prepares to loft a homemade bird feeder. Linda Sue Stith (*upper right*) smiles an optimistic Brownie smile. *Lower right:* This Brownie instructs Daisies in cookery. Note the tri-state council patch on her sash.**

es which are sewn onto their uniforms, sometimes by the girls themselves. During their last year as Brownie Girl Scouts, they start planning to become Junior Girl Scouts by working on activities specific to that goal. When they are ready to become Junior Girl Scouts, Brownie Girl Scouts receive the 'Bridge to Juniors' patch, a crescent-shaped patch that fits above their Brownie Girl Scout patches.

Brownie Girl Scouts continue the Girl Scout program activities in the five broad interest areas: the World of Well-Being, the World of People, the World of Today and Tomorrow, the World of the Arts, and the World of the Out-of-Doors.

In the World of Well-Being a Brownie Girl Scout learns that she is special to the world, that her health and happiness influence others to be that way, too. A new troop that

may not yet know each other well can become well acquainted, by asking the rest of the troop questions about likes, dislikes, feelings, favorite things—all questions from the World of Well-Being. The special sisterhood of Girl Scouts and Girl Guides worldwide becomes apparent to Brownie Girl Scouts when they share themselves with others and learn that many similarities bind them to each other.

Brownie Girl Scouts learn that their bodies are like complicated machines. They learn that keeping their bodies healthy is important to feeling good. Brownie Girl Scouts talk about daily health habits such as eating right, maintaining body cleanliness and exercising, plus the importance of regular preventive medicine. They might make puppets to act out skits about these things, or play games that stress physical fitness, or enjoy aerobic dances to understand the World of Well-Being by experiencing it. Brownie Girl Scouts love active games and there is no limit to how they can study the World of Well-Being, as long as they also remember that their actions affect others and therefore must consider the effects of their play. Sometimes quiet games might be more in order, but they still can emphasize 'well-being.' Brownie Girl Scouts are fond of 'The Shape Game,' (recalling objects on a tray after a short glimpse of the tray), which was one of Juliette Low's favorite games too.

The concept of 'home' is shared in the troop. 'Home' means something different to each Brownie Girl Scout, but each 'home' shares similarities. Although their outward configurations are different, a home is usually a nice place to live if it is filled with happiness; it makes people feel good. Brownie Girl Scouts discuss ways to make their homes filled with smiles.

Community helpers contribute to the World of Well-Being, and Brownie Girl Scouts learn who they are and how they help. A troop may take a field trip to the local fire station or health-care facility, or they might enjoy a visit from a health professional or a crossing guard. Brownie Girl Scouts can also learn to take some responsibility for themselves by listing emergency phone numbers and practicing making a telephone call in an emergency. They can take turns making the calls and being the person who answers—a learning experience that is also fun. The Brownie Girl Scout Handbook offers many suggestions for activities in the World of Well-Being, including fire safety and first aid.

Ethnic diversity enriches the sisterhood of Girl Scouts of the USA. *Left:* A merry-go-round Brownie Girl Scout. *Above:* A Brownie Girl Scout and her troop leader.

Through the World of People, Brownies Girl Scouts become aware that their world is ever-expanding, that it is no longer just the family or the classroom or the neighborhood. They begin to realize that their experience in Girl Scouting has already broadened their scope and that Brownie Girl Scouts can explore the World of People to understand it better. To begin the exploration, they start close to home. They discuss family heritage, their own special backgrounds and family stories. Then they progress to the community level—how their community got its name, what it looked like 10—or even 200—years before.

Brownie Girl Scouts share ideas for friendship—realizing already how important friends are. They learn how to *be* a friend as well as friendship's gestures. Activities based on friendly gestures to others are popular with Brownie Girl Scouts—giving handmade articles to others, inviting others into the troop activities, helping the com-

BROWNIE GIRL SCOUT TRY-ITS

People of the World

Play

Girl Scout Ways

Outdoor Happenings

Movers

Outdoor Fun

Plants and Animals

Math Shapes

Science Magic

Dance

Music

Sports

Food Fun

Colors and Shapes

Puppets, Dolls and Toys

munity in different ways, planting living things or visiting people who are not able to move about easily.

Brownie Girl Scouts may share cultural or religious celebrations with others in their troop who may not have the same background. In this way Brownie Girl Scouts can enjoy each other's cultures and expand their knowledge in the World of People. The wider world also includes the international family of Girl Scouting. Brownie Girl Scouts can enjoy making a *krathong* (a floating Thai ceremonial vessel) or play *San Sereni* (A Puerto Rican singing game) with as much enjoyment as their sister scouts in those parts of the world. Related activities, such as tasting foods from these faraway places, can complement the experience and further provide the basis for discussing world food needs—how they are met or not met, and what Brownie Girl Scouts can do to help.

Brownie Girl Scouts discover the World of Today and Tomorrow by exploring and experimenting. How daring the exploration or how scientific the experiment is usually guided by the troop leader, who must be sure that the activities for the troop are, first of all, safe. Suggestions for this activity area are found in the Brownie Girl Scout Handbook. Certainly an equal number of ideas may be suggested by members of the troop, because Brownie Girl Scouts are full of ideas.

Brownie Girl Scouts prepare themselves for the World of Tomorrow by discussing what they want to be when they are adults and playing 'Who Says So?'—a game that tests different ideas of what constitutes 'women's work.'

Above: **These Brownies are playing musical glasses.** *Right:* **Mrs Janeen Sherrill receives a contribution of homemade blocks for the Fort Lewis, Washington Child Care Center from Manuela Miller, Diana Ballard and Colleen Gardner of Girl Scout Troop 668 (in 1974).** *Overleaf:* **Junior Girl Scouts share a giggle.**

The World of the Arts teaches that appreciating art is more than just viewing pieces in a museum or attending a play, and Brownie Girl Scouts learn that they exist within the World of the Arts—seeing, feeling and listening. Art is all around us, and learning to appreciate it also teaches Brownie Girl Scouts to appreciate the people who made the art whether they lived 'long ago and far away' or around the corner.

Brownie Girl Scouts discuss elements of art using its particular language (rhythm, pattern, texture, line, space) and practice using these elements in their own art projects. A troop leader can encourage the artist within each Brownie Girl Scout, whether or not the leader is an artist herself, because all the efforts of the leader aim to encourage each girl to develop her fullest potential. The leader also encourages Brownies to take part in the joy of books—from appreciating their manufacture by leading a field trip to a bindery, to sharing the printed page in a poetry reading. By encouraging Brownies Girl Scouts to write, the troop leader fosters a love of language and may even be fanning the flames of nascent talent.

The World of the Out-of-Doors makes discovery of the out-of-doors popular with Brownie Girl Scouts. Activities may take the form of hikes and campouts or discussions of ecology and the food chain. Girl Scouts speak of learning about the environment and taking care of it in the Girl Scout Law:'to use resources wisely' and 'to protect and improve the world around me.'

Brownie Girl Scouts can discover the World of the Out-of-Doors by bird watching, observing the weather, planting trees or seeds, or looking for the constellations.

The World of the Out-of-Doors may mean travel for Brownie Girl Scouts. They can discuss plans (and alternative plans) and try to 'Be Prepared' for the trip. Safety rules and good outdoor manners remind Brownies of their special role as Girl Scouts. A Girl Scout can use the sun or stars to find directions, she knows how to follow a trail from markers and she knows about mapping. Girl Scouts

may begin to learn some of these skills when they are Brownie Girl Scouts.

Girl Scouts may have their first camping experience as Brownie Girl Scouts, and they share responsibilities for planning the experience. Their Brownie Girl Scout Handbook suggests ways to ensure that everyone has a hand in planning so the trip will be enjoyable for everyone, and that everyone has responsibilities so no one is overloaded with chores. The Handbook gives practical lists of equipment, diagrams and safety tips. The same lists that serve Brownie Girl Scouts in their first camping experience would also serve as reminders to the seasoned camper, because the lists represent the kind of practical knowhow for which Scouts (both boys and girls) are known.

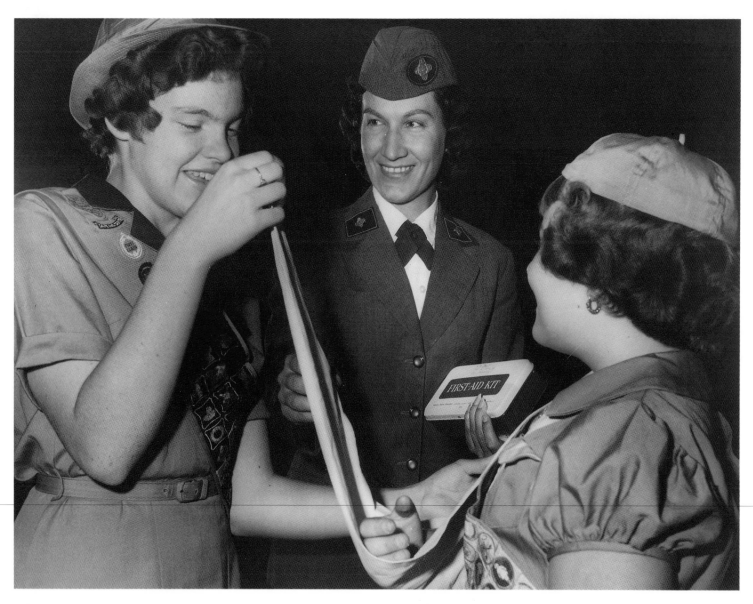

Above: Girl Scouts of another era practice first aid. *Below:* The Air Force, and other armed services, often sponsor Scout troops. *Upper Right:* US Army Maj Gen Bert A David enjoys a display at the 1974 Okinawa District Girl Scout Expo. *Lower Right:* Brownies engage in sisterhood-oriented fun.

JUNIOR GIRL SCOUTS

Girls from 9 to 11 years old (or in fourth through sixth grades) can become Junior Girl Scouts. A girl who has previously been a Brownie Girl Scout becomes a Junior Girl Scout in a 'fly-up', or bridging ceremony in which she receives a Brownie Wings emblem (showing that she was once a Brownie Girl Scout) and a Girl Scout pin. She may continue to wear her Bridge to Juniors patch, and she renews the Girl Scout Promise.

A girl who has not been a Brownie Girl Scout makes the Promise and receives her Girl Scout pin at an investiture ceremony. Junior Girl Scouts wear a long- or short-sleeved print blouse with solid green bolero vest and skirt or trousers. They might also add a solid green baseball cap or wool beret. Their official camp uniform is a solid green polo shirt and shorts.

Until 1987, the Junior Girl Scouts program shared the same handbook as the Brownie Girl Scouts program, and therefore their activities were similar. Junior Girl Scouts, however, because of their greater age explore career activities more deeply, in ways that allow them to investigate fields that interest them, and continue the Worlds of Interest activities they enjoyed as Brownie Girl Scouts.

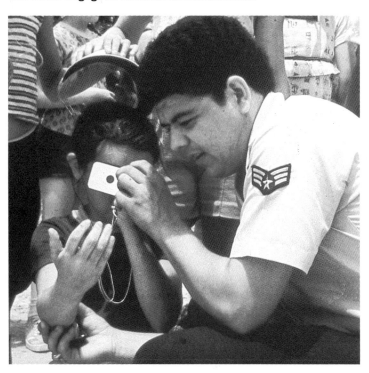

Junior Girl Scouts can earn a wide variety of badges in such areas as arts and crafts, camping, health and safety, sports and community service. They may also earn the Junior Aide Patch and the Bridging patch that shows activity preparing them for Cadette Girl Scouts, the next Girl Scout level.

Junior Girl Scouts show their advancement in responsible citizenship by governing their troop by the patrol system, steering committee or town meeting. Their adult leader (still a volunteer) continues to supply a sense of direction and helps the troop toward agreement on shared goals. The adult leader sees that each member understands her own part in reaching goals and keeps an eye on individual progress and on relationships between members. The adult leader remains responsible for the troop's records and finances although she may be assisted in leadership by older Girl Scouts or other adults.

Badges are designed to encourage girls to investigate and develop skills in a wide variety of subject areas and are grouped according to the five Girl Scout Worlds of Interest. In each world the Girl Scout can work towards Dabbler badges—badges with green or tan backgrounds. Green badges are for girls with less experience; tan are for girls with some skill in the subject area.

Although a great number of badges exist in Girl Scouting, if girls in a troop are interested in a subject for which no badge exists, they can develop a special badge. The

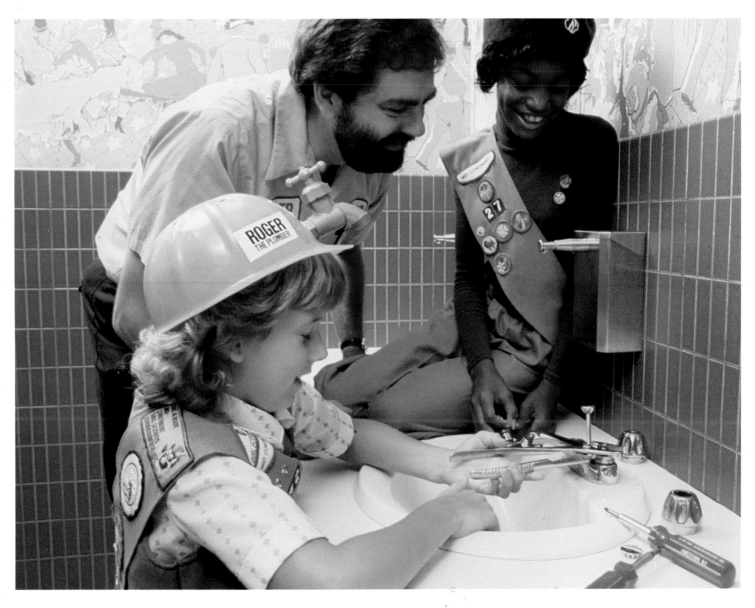

local council approves the subject, and the girls develop the activities related to their special badge with the guidance of their troop leader. The girls then design and make their own badge insignia, which only they may wear.

A troop leader knows that recognition badges and signs are meant to encourage troop members in their development. Recognitions are meant for enrichment—they are not essential. A well-balanced troop program is the goal of the troop—not the accumulation of patches and signs. The earning of recognitions is an exciting extension of the Girl Scout program. Recognitions provide opportunities for creative thinking in Girl Scouts and encourage them to share their learning with others.

CADETTE GIRL SCOUTS

Girls 12 to 14 years old (or in the seventh, eighth, or ninth grades) may become Cadette Girl Scouts. Cadette Girl Scouts wear a green plaid blouse with solid green vest and skirt. They also might wear solid green trousers as an optional part of their official uniform. The Cadette Girl Scouting program stresses career exploration in such areas as the arts, business, health, science and social services. Cadette Girl Scouts learn what training

Junior Girl Scouts enjoy a wide variety of badge-eligible activities: baseball (upper left), tongue-in-cheek ballet (lower left), plumbing and other fix-it skills (above), and giving nature lessons (below). In addition to existing badges, new ones can be developed for suitable activities.

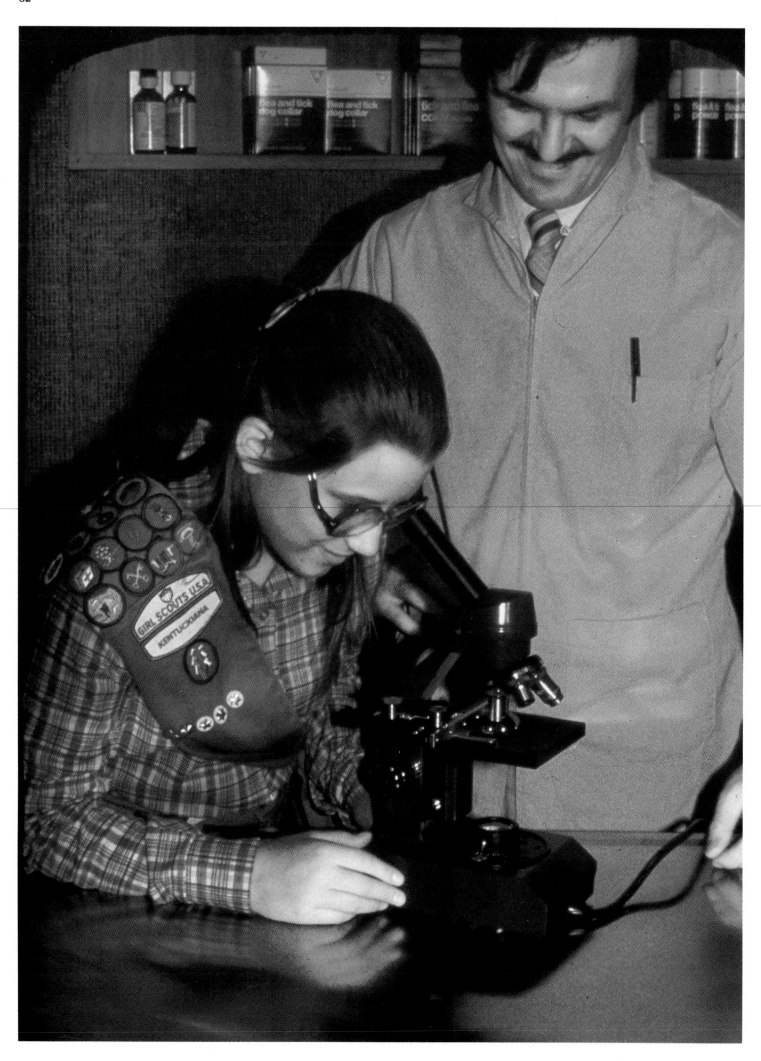

63

Left: **This Cadette Girl Scout engages one of the increasingly complex activities that coincide with the higher age brackets of Scouting.** *Above:* **Girl Scouts learn care and responsibility in planning their activities, which include service projects.**

and education are required for each career and begin to evaluate their own interests and abilities in relation to career choices. Consistent with the Girl Scout message, Cadette Girl Scouts do not limit themselves to exploring only 'women's work'; they develop their own potential to the fullest in order to bring their dreams into reality. No one knows how many girls make lasting career decisions at junior-high age, but Cadette Girl Scouts are encouraged to 'look wide' for their dreams, and the experience they gain as Cadettes fosters the self-confidence to make knowledgeable decisions in later years.

Cadette Girl Scouts gain their experiences in decision-making first hand. When planning an activity, Cadette Girl Scouts are right there at the onset organizing for action. After they've set a goal, the steps to reaching it are laid down too. For example, if their goal as a troop is to camp overnite, they must take the steps to reserve the campsite, check the first-aid kit and arrange for transportation. The knowledge gained from this planning process relates directly to any long-range goal—whether the goal is to be a NASA engineer, to teach at a university or to join the diplomatic corps.

Cadette Girl Scouts practice delegating responsibility, making sure that the load is balanced effectively. Duplication of effort or overload on one person is eliminated when responsibility and labor are equitably divided. Several plans for charting a course of action are suggested in the Cadette Girl Scout handbook, *You Make the Difference.*

These plans are sensible and effective tools for reaching any goal. In the forms of 'a shopping list', 'the big picture', 'the countdown' and a 'long-run calendar', steps in planning are suggested that are practical and thought-provoking. Cadette Girl Scouts (or adults) can use these tools to help them carry through an activity that is long or short range, close to home or far away, large or small.

Records need to be stored somewhere besides memory. Cadette Girl Scouts learn that record keeping is important to reaching their goals, and that it keeping can be an on-going project or a specific activity: it serves to mark progress and to evaluate outcome. Records are especially helpful when the troop wants to recall past efforts and evaluations, answer questions about time and money, plan ahead and monitor progress, make agreements and share results, and pass on information to new members. Planning an agenda, taking notes and building a budget are methods of record keeping that Cadette Girl Scouts can use during the time they are Scouts as well as when they are adults.

Evaluating a project usually occurs naturally if it has been successful—people have no trouble recognizing success. It's evaluating a less-than-completely-successful project that may be troublesome. Cadette Girl Scouts learn not to label their project as 'failures,' because even bad experiences can be built upon by trying again. Using Girl Scout program terms, they can evaluate whether they have acquired new skills, contributed to society, learned more about themselves, related to others, balanced active and quiet pursuits, varied activities for all five Worlds of Interest or specialized in one, explored their roles and potential as women, interacted with other Girl Scouts, learned about another culture or had fun. Cadette Girl Scouts using this evaluation list realize that even a project that did not sparkle has helped them achieve more than one of their Girl Scout aims.

Cadette Girl Scouts are recognized for their achievements, with certificates and patches in a wide variety of choices from auto mechanics to fashion. Their projects may be carried out individually or in groups. Many of their badge recognitions are dabbler badges which encourage a wide variety of interests. Cadette Girl Scouts may work on the Girl Scout Challenges (discussed in the Senior Girl Scout section of this manuscript) and may begin work toward earning the Girl Scout Silver Award.

Cadette Girl Scout activities continue the Worlds of Interest activities of the Girl Scout program and are expanded to encompass the interests of its older membership.

Cadette Girl Scouts who are at least 12 years old may request a pen pal from the International Postbox, thereby contributing to (and benefitting from) the worldwide sisterhood of Girl Guides and Girl Scouts.

Effective fund-raising for various causes is a real possibility for Cadette Girl Scouts, who may hold a car wash, put on a show or sell gifts to raise funds for activities. Choosing a worthy activity, planning a project and fulfilling the plans are practices in self-government and responsibility, as well as service.

To expand their own horizons, Cadette Girl Scouts might investigate careers that for years were male dominated. If a Cadette Girl Scout is interested in medicine, for example, she might volunteer as a local hospital guide or aide and see firsthand the work of doctors. If she is interested in a career in broadcast journalism, she might interview someone working in that field or visit a local television station. Cadette Girl Scouts might choose to investigate in Challenge groups rather than working independently.

Cadette Girl Scouts continue to be physically active and participate in outdoor activities—camping, swimming and hiking are normal activities for busy Cadette Girl Scouts.

Upper right: **A knowledgeable leader can teach her troop many skills, and can further aid them toward rounding out their Girl Scouting competence by using patience, care and preparedness in instructing them.** *Lower right:* **These Senior Girl Scouts are learning broadcasting as a possible career skill.**

SENIOR GIRL SCOUTS

Senior Girl Scouts are from 14 to 17 years old, or in the ninth through twelfth grades. The Senior Girl Scout program offers further opportunities for career exploration, self improvement and community service. Senior Girl Scouts may themselves volunteer to work with younger troops. They continue to earn recognitions and may achieve the highest award in Girl Scouting, the Girl Scout Gold Award.

Senior Girl Scouts wear a blue plaid blouse, green vest and green skirt or trousers. Their official camp uniform consists of a pale blue polo shirt and green shorts emblazoned with the Girl Scout trefoil.

Cadette Girl Scouts and Senior Girl Scouts work on two challenges: The Challenge of Being a Girl Scout and The Challenge of Living the Promise and Law. Each challenge asks the Girl Scout to deepen her understanding of herself, of others, and to find the unique ways that she can contribute to the well-being of her community. Completing a challenge may take a year; it is not a one-step process. Each challenge encompasses four preps (preparation steps) before the actual challenge.

In accepting The Challenge of Being a Girl Scout, the Scout's first prep is to know about Girl Scouting. She can answer specific questions about Girl Scouting that involve research into Girl Scout history or organization. She can answer 11 specific questions about Girl Scouting before she chooses her challenge activity, questions such as 'What is WAGGGS?' 'In what ways are your religious beliefs similar to the Girl Scout Promise and Law?' 'How did Girl Scouting begin?' or 'Who are your council's delegates to the National Council session and what do they do there?' Then she designs or selects an activity that shows she understands the purpose and history of Scouting.

Completing the second prep means that the Girl Scout knows herself. She has completed a set of questions such as 'What do I like to do best?' 'What can I do well?' 'What new things have I tried lately?' or 'How well do I keep physically fit?' After answering these questions, a Senior Girl Scout might find that she is very interested in sports but has limited herself to just a few favorites. In this case,

GIRL SCOUT TROOP CRESTS

Bluebell · Bluebird · Bluebonnet · Brown Pansy · Buttercup · Cardinal Bird · Clover Leaf · Daffodil · Daisy · Dogwood · Forget-Me-Not · Lily of the Valley

Mountain Laurel · Pine Cone · Pine Tree · Poppy · Purple Pansy · Purple Violet · Red Rose · Robin · Star of Bethlehem · White Rose · Wild Rose · Morning Glory Crest

Above: Girl Scout skill levels rise with their age bracket—these Seniors are learning fine carpentry. *Left:* The whole team goes 'up for it' in this game of volleyball. Scouting interests range from the difficult intricacy of ballet (*right*) to the dangerous intricacy of ropewalking across a gorge (*overleaf*). In any situation Girl Scouts are well prepared.

she might choose to try a new sport and to develop some proficiency at it. She might have been terrific at competitive team sports, but had never tried a singular non-competitive sport such as cross-country skiing. She will have to spend at least five hours in her new activity, so she will probably discuss her choice with her adult leader to make sure it is a good learning experience for her. When she has completed her exploration into a new activity, she will know herself better and will also know that she has tried to improve herself.

In the third prep, the Girl Scout questions the way she relates to others and completes an activity in which her skills in this area are demonstrated. Some questions for the third prep are 'What ways do I show friendship?' 'How do I give encouragement to others?' or 'Whom do I go to if I need help?' Our Senior Girl Scout may find that she likes people, but is acquainted with only a limited age range. Her activity for the third prep may be to host a coffee hour for the senior citizens group at her church, opening herself up in friendliness and showing that she cares for people who are far older than herself.

At the fourth prep, the Girl Scout evaluates her values and how she came to hold them. Our Girl Scout examines her values by answering such questions as 'What do I feel most strongly about?' 'What values are hardest for me to live by?' 'Have I ever consented to do something I really didn't believe in?' and 'What parts of the Girl Scout Law

Whether a Scout is teaching or being taught; in a singalong group (*above*), or in a one-on-one swimming lesson (*left*); sisterhood is always at the center of Scout activity. These Scouts (*upper right*) embark on their adventure with a qualified guide to show them the way through the 'white water.'

am I able to act upon regularly?' She then plans a Girl Scouts' Own, a ceremony that demonstrates the Girl Scout Promise and Law. Our Senior Girl Scout intends her ceremony to be balanced between joy and solemnity, and for her Girl Scouts' Own decides to invite her troop to meet the senior citizens group at her church. She plans to open the ceremony with a reading of the Girl Scout Promise and Law, then asks selected persons (both young and old) to speak about their perceptions of Girl Scouting. She will then encourage the older people to talk about their own lives. The combination of thoughtful reminiscence and the assembly of a widespread age group would most likely produce an uplifting Girl Scouts' Own ceremony. Our Girl Scout must also make sure that all the elements to produce the ceremony—invitations and physical arrangements—are taken care of. This example would be quite an elaborate Girl Scouts' Own. Another Girl Scout at the fourth prep might choose to prepare a much simpler ceremony for a smaller group.

The Challenge of Being a Girl Scout uses what the Scout has learned in the four prep sections. Her challenge

is to do something for her community in which she gives of herself and which makes a significant impact on the community. The challenge puts into practice everything the Scout has learned from Scouting—from selecting her goal through evaluating how successfully she has reached it. From completing the four preps, our Girl Scout has found that she is interested in the welfare of older people. Her challenge, then, might be to arrange a program to help senior citizens from her church who are stranded without transportation. She would not necessarily drive them around herself, but might contact and recruit volunteers for this type of service. Then she could compile a directory of volunteers for the senior citizens to call upon when they need a ride.

The Challenge of Living the Promise and Law has five sections. A Girl Scout who has met this challenge has shown that she has made the Promise and Law a part of her daily life. She may complete the first four steps in any order. At the end of each step, she and her leader decide if it has been satisfactorily completed.

First, she demonstrates her knowledge about Girl Scouting in an activity far beyond troop level. She might become a delegate to a national Girl Scout event.

Second, she tries to know herself better by comparing other people's impressions of her with her own impression of herself, and then she designs a self-development plan of at least two months' duration—it might include the learning of a new skill or the expansion of an existing potential—and then evaluates the progress she has made at this second step toward the challenge.

Third, she examines her relationship to others by completing a chart that helps her profile her skills in relating to other people—her family members, friends, men, women, boys, girls, people of other ethnic or religious groups and children. She examines her profile and summarizes a plan to increase her skills in relating to others.

Fourth, the Girl Scout develops a summary of her values by keeping a journal for a minimum of two months. She makes notes on how she lives up to the Girl Scout Promise and each part of the Girl Scout Law. She summarizes her journal and what she has discovered from it. She thinks about the question, 'Did you find that what you actually say and do matches what you say you believe?'

Fifth, the Girl Scout is challenged to design, develop and carry out a project that will benefit her community. Her project must show others what she values and should be in an area she cares about deeply, and about which she feels she will continue to care about. Her interest in the welfare of older people might have grown so great that she will decide to expand her transportation project beyond her church, to include the whole community. After she

Left: While fun is an important part of Girl Scout life, the Scout program emphasis progresses from the first steps of exploration undertaken by Daisy Girl Scouts to the complex, responsible and even rigorous projects undertaken by Senior Girl Scouts.

Above: These jubilant Senior Girl Scouts show their council identification strips—a blue and white patch on girl *at left,* who also wears a gold six-pointed membership star; and a black pin on the girl *at right,* who also wears an equestrian interests pin.

INTERESTS PROJECT BADGES

Photography · Leadership · Dabbler · Child Care · Creative Cooking · Emergency Preparedness · Fashion/Fitness Makeup · Sports · Skills For Living · Tune in to Well-Being · Dabbler · Community Time Capsule · Global Understanding

Travel · Do You Get The Message · Heritage Hunt · Dabbler · Auto Maintenance · Career Exploration · Energy Awareness · Money Management · Plant Culture · High-Tech Communication · Dabbler · Folk Arts · Music

Visual Arts · The Play's The Thing · Invitation To The Dance · Dabbler · Camping · Eco-Action · Outdoor Survival · Water Sports · Wildlife · Horse Sense · Paddle, Pole and Roll · Our Own Council's · Or Own Troop's

Above: **Juliette Low sessions provide special arrangements for Disabled Scouts activities.** *Right:* **This charming young lady reveals considerable inner strength, like many Disabled Scouts.**

completes her project, she and her leader evaluate it and decide whether her challenge has been completed.

The activities of Senior Girl Scouts take into consideration their greater levels of capability. Service projects may be more intense or comprehensive than those attempted by younger Girl Scouts. While younger Girl Scouts may visit a child care center or 'help out' at a center, Senior Girl Scouts might establish one in a needed area. Responsibility, self-improvement and service by Senior Girl Scouts is intrinsic to their function and, if they have sufficient experience in Scouting, these qualities are second nature to them.

When Senior Girl Scouts have an interest in a topic, they are encouraged to follow it. Their interests may rest in their own communities or range far beyond the troop. Many Senior Girl Scouts feel a responsibility to encourage Scouting for younger girls and may lend their skills in leadership to a younger troop.

They are encouraged to set their goals high. Participating in a national conference or event might be the goal of one Senior Girl Scout, or becoming a delegate from the United States to an international event might be the goal of another. Always stressed in setting a goal is the route to reaching it; the opportunities and rewards gathered along the route may be as important as reaching the goal itself.

GIRL SCOUTING FOR THE DISABLED

Girl Scouts of the USA is open to *all* girls and recognizes that one in ten American children has a disability. Girls who have disabilities are welcomed into Girl Scout troops whether the rest of the troop is without disabilities or not. Girl Scouting attempts to serve girls with special needs in two basic ways—as members of a regular troop or in special troops made up entirely of girls with the same disability. The first troop of disabled girls was formed in 1917 in New York City.

Whenever possible, girls with disabilities are included in troops with other girls. Troop leaders recognize that such a girl is more *like* the rest of the troop than different from them. These leaders focus on each girl's strengths and try to maximize them by building on each step along the way. Other troop members have the opportunity to welcome a disabled member into their circle, and really get to know a girl who is slightly different from themselves. The give-and-take atmosphere of a Girl Scout troop fosters friendship and learning for everyone involved.

The Girl Scouts USA program offers guidelines to troop leaders who may be unfamiliar with the nature of various disabilities. When children and adults have the opportunity to learn about one another, they can participate and work together comfortably. The opportunity to work with a disabled troop member might also be a learning experience for the adult leader who wants to be able to help enrich the lives of each of her troop members. By including a girl with a disability, the troop leader has a special opportunity to foster the best qualities in each girl as well as in herself. Open discussion is but one of the ways that all troop members can learn from each other. Often, children with disabilities are knowledgeable about their conditions and are willing and effective teachers.

Some activities of the troop may be adapted to include the needs of its disabled members but, since adaptations for individual abilities and limitations is part of the normal course of events in any troop, the adaptations are not obstacles to an enriching Girl Scout program. The program materials are designed with individualization in mind. They allow for differences in community patterns and resources, leader styles and abilities, and the range of experiences that girls themselves bring to their troop.

Many Girl Scout activities have no set requirements. The girls and their leader decide on the things they'd like to do, based on their interests. For these activities, adaptations are not a problem—the requirements are personalized; they are not simplified. Other adaptations for geography or climate, available local resources or special opportunities are regularly made for the Girl Scout program. When adaptations are made to accommodate the needs of the disabled, they remain in line with the purpose of the activity. Possible ways to adapt include changing the method, modifying the activity or substituting an activity. For example, rather than making an on-site visit, a troop may see a film or invite a speaker to their meeting. A blind Girl Scout might devise a way to mark poisonous plants in a way recognizable to blind persons (rather than telling how to recognize the plants) and thereby earn the Rambler badge.

Girls who are severely disabled are often members of a special Girl Scout troop made up entirely of girls with the same or a similar disability. Usually these girls attend a special school, and often their troops meet at school. Teachers or other professionals at the school may be recruited to be troop leaders because of their knowledge related to the disability. Special troops are always encouraged to participate with other troops in the Girl Scout council, so that their Girl Scout experience is as rich as possible. In Girl Scouting, all girls can feel good about themselves, have fun and learn through their experiences. The ultimate aim in Girl Scouting is to help girls develop positive attitudes about themselves and others, and there are an infinite number of ways to reach that goal.

In 1985 girls with disabilities participated in international projects that took place in the United Kingdom, Finland, Germany, Jamaica, Canada and Japan. An event at the Girl Scouts' National Center West (in Wyoming), for girls with and without hearing impairments, involved sign language sessions, backpacking, archaeology, finish, geology and crafts.

The national Girl Scout organization conducted a training workshop called 'Serving Girls with Disabilities' for representatives from Girl Scout councils in 1985. The organization discussed its experience and shared its expertise at The President's Committee on Employment of the Handicapped annual conference.

JULIETTE LOW WORLD FRIENDSHIP FUND

A few months after Juliette Low died in 1927, the Girl Scouts of the United States started the Juliette Low World Friendship Fund to honor their founder and her vision of worldwide friendship. Girl Scouts in the United States give money to the fund every year—usually on Juliette Low's birthday or on Thinking Day (22 February), the birthday of Lord and Olave Baden-Powell.

Part of the funds raised can be used to send older Girl Scouts to other countries where they can visit and learn more about how people in those places live, or the funds can be used to bring Girl Guides to the United States. The rest goes to the Thinking Day Fund, administered by the World Association, in which it is used for international projects that promote friendship between girls of all nationalities, races and religions.

Girl Scouts of all ages can donate to the Juliette Low World Friendship Fund as individuals or as troops. They might raise the money in such ways as through bake sales or recycling drives, or they may give their personal allowances in the name of international friendship. Girl Scouts show in this way that they really care about people—even if the people live in countries far away.

GIRL GUIDING IN THE UNITED KINGDOM

Approximately 700,000 girls belong to the Girl Guides Association, which was founded in 1910. Over the years, millions of girls have made the Guide promise and taken part in the range of activities in the Guide program aimed at developing individual character, self-reliance, self discipline and a desire to help others.

The aim of the Association is to provide a program that embraces a wide range of leisure-time activities and interests that, while enjoyable in themselves, have an underlying educational purpose—to develop individual character based on the values expressed in the Guide Promise and Law.

The activities of the Girl Guides Association are reviewed and updated periodically to offer contemporary choices for its membership. Its lively program covers a wide area of interests, from outdoor ventures, to home activities, to modern technology. Guiding is a leisure activity with a purpose. Almost any interest can be followed within Guiding, and in such a way that it encourages development of individual talents and skills—for both leaders and team members.

England is where the Scout movement began, and therefore the history of the Girl Guides is that of the entire movement, which is outlined at the beginning of this book. The work begun by Robert Baden-Powell, expanded by his sister, Agnes, and continued by his wife, Olave, has changed the world. For their work many official and prestigious honors were bestowed upon them (Nobel Peace Prize nomination, commemorative coins, etc), but among their finest honors must be the continuation of the movement that began over 80 years ago.

Lord Baden-Powell remarked on this continuation in his last message to the Girl Guides:

'My Dear Guides—This is just a farewell note to you, the last that you will have from me. It is just to remind you when I have passed on that your business in life is to be happy and to make others happy. That sounds comfortable and easy, doesn't it? You begin making other people happy by doing good turns to them. You need not worry about making yourselves happy, as you will very soon find that that comes by itself, when you make other people happy, it makes you happy too. . . . I am sure God means us to be happy in this life. He has given us a world to live in that is full of beauties and wonders, and He has given

Left: **Brownie Girl Scouts 'uphold the globe' in an opening event at the 25th World Conference on the campus of Marymount College, at Tarrytown, New York in July of 1984.** *Above:* **In this 1932 photo, Chief Guide Lady Olave Baden-Powell wears the Dame Grand Cross, which she was awarded by the British Empire.**

us not only eyes to see them but minds to understand them if we only have the sense to look at them in that light. We can enjoy bright sunshine and glorious views. We can see beauty in the flowers. We can watch with wonder how the seed produces the young plant which grows to a flower which in its turn will replace other

flowers as they die off . . . By giving out love and happiness . . . you will gain for yourselves . . . return love . . . and there is nothing better in this world. You will find that Heaven is not the kind of happiness somewhere up in the skies after you are dead but right here and now in this world in your own home. So guide others to happiness and you will bring happiness to yourselves and by doing this you will be doing what God wants of you.'

The thrust of Lord Baden-Powell's message remains relevant. In emphasizing service to others, he might have been summarizing the Girl Guides of today. Specific activities may have been molded to appeal to contemporary girls, but the roots of their traditions took hold over eight decades ago.

The governing body of the Girl Guides Association is the Council. Day-to-day management of the Association's affairs rests with the Executive Committee of the Council, consisting of not fewer than five—or more than twelve—elected members and several ex-officio members. A General Secretary is the senior salaried official of the Association, and acts as secretary to both the Council and the Executive Committee of the Council.

The national headquarters of the Girl Guides Association is in London. The Association publishes four periodicals: 'The Brownie' weekly, 'Today's Guide' monthly, 'Guiding' monthly, and 'The Trefoil' quarterly. The Association also publishes official handbooks for each age group, and a variety of brochures, leaflets, charts and cassettes.

For administrative purposes the United Kingdom is divided into nine countries and regions: North West England, North East England, Midlands, Anglia, South West England, London and South East England, Scotland,

Wales and Ulster. Each has its own headquarters with a General Secretary and small staff. The countries and regions are further subdivided into counties, divisions, districts and individual units.

Uniformed adult leaders of Brownie, Guide or Ranger Guide Units are known as Guiders. Leaders who are responsible for a number of units at district, division or country level are Commissioners. Other uniformed adults may be specialist advisers, trainers, secretaries, etc.

Women of eighteen years of age or over may become Guiders. No special qualifications are required except membership in the Girl Guide Association (including making the Guide Promise). A Guider may spend up to a year working for her Adult Leader's Certificate at a district level before taking on a unit. Some women may not be able to take on the full commitment of becoming Guiders; they may register as Unit Helpers and assist in a variety of ways at unit level.

Girls from 15 to 18 years of age may participate in the Young Leader's Scheme and work with younger members of the Association. They do not have to be Ranger Guides to participate in this scheme.

Training for leaders takes place at the local level or at official training centers in England, Scotland, Ulster and Wales where weekend courses are arranged throughout the year. The training courses include specialist subjects in the arts or outdoor activities. Any Guider in the United Kingdom or the Commonwealth may apply to attend the weekend training courses.

Any girl or woman who is able to make the Guide Promise may join the Girl Guides Association. A Ranger Guide makes a further commitment to be of service to her community. Girls of any race or religion may voluntarily join

Left: **Exuberant international Guide and Scout delegates walk with their Chief, Olave Baden-Powell (*center*) at the 3rd World Conference held in Foxlease, England in 1924.** *Above:* **The faces of the 1909 1st Kidderminster Guide Company still symbolize the diversity of the world wide Scout and Guide movement.** *Right, at left:* **Nesta Ashworth formed the first Lone Guide company in 1908, and won the Silver Fish Award in 1911 (*photo*). 'BP's' sister, Agnes Baden-Powell is *at center*.**

the Girl Guides. Handicapped girls are encouraged to join regular local units or special units for handicapped girls, which have been in existence since the Scout Movement's earliest days.

Some girls, because of work or studies, may be isolated from local Girl Guide units. They may become Guides and keep in touch by correspondence through the Lone Scheme.

In 1983 there were nearly 815,000 uniformed members of the Girl Guides Association in the United Kingdom. This number included over 400,000 Brownie Guides; 300,000 Guides; 17,000 Ranger Guides; 6,600 Young Leaders (working with Brownies or Guides); and 64,000 Guiders (adult leaders). An additional 35,832 non-uniformed members came from Trefoil Guild members, Unit Helpers, Link and other Guide Clubs.

Among the luminaries who support the Girl Guides Association are Her Majesty Queen Elizabeth, The Queen Mother and Her Royal Highness Princess Margaret, Countess of Snowden. As girls, Queen Elizabeth and her sister Margaret both enjoyed Girl Guide membership, an activity that allowed them, at least once a week, to be 'like everyone else.'

Today Queen Elizabeth and The Queen Mother are patrons of the Girl Guides Association, and Princess Margaret is the organization's president.

Left: **Guides at Matlock Station, Derbyshire warmly greet a chief patron—Her Majesty Queen Elizabeth.** *Above:* **North Yorkshire Guides and Brownies meet their association president, Princess Margaret.** *Right:* **A Ray Charles lyric adorns the camp t-shirts that these 'splashy' Scouts wear.**

Princess Margaret launched the Girl Guides' 75th anniversary celebration in 1985 by presenting lighted candles to delegates from each county and region and from British Guides in foreign countries.

The lights were carried around their counties and regions by transportation arranged by ingenious Rangers—by foot, bicycle, horseback, boat and etc. At each stop the Rangers lit more candles. By the end of the week-long celebration, the flame from Her Royal Highness's candle had lit almost three million others. Many of those candles decorated thousands of birthday cakes celebrating the 75th anniversary throughout the United Kingdom. Some dedicated individuals commemorated the occasion by undertaking 75 Good Turns.

Many adults wish to support the Girl Guides and Boy Scouts Movement in ways other than in leadership roles. Several organizations exist which welcome their support.

The Trefoil Guild is open to adults who wish to support Girl Guiding but who are unable to be actively connected to it. Women over the age of eighteen may give their support in this way.

Link is an organization for young adults who wish to maintain an association with the Guide Movement by pursuing some form of service. Link gives priority to international activities.

The Scout and Guide Graduate Association (SAGGA) promotes Scout and Guide cooperation and supports Scout and Guide Clubs in higher educational institutions. Anyone who supports SAGGA's aims may become a member.

The Student Scout and Guide Organization (SSAGO) forms Scout and Guide clubs in universities and colleges, and provides a variety of activities for students who wish to maintain renew or acquire an interest in Scouting or Guiding.

The Local Association is formed of people who help Commissioners and Guiders with administrative work at the local level. This association assists relationships with local authorities, the public, and parents and helps to provide local financial support.

The Supporters Committee is a group of adults interested in giving support to a unit or related units. The Committee may support both Scout and Guide units.

BROWNIE GUIDES

Brownie Guides are the youngest members of The Girl Guides Association. Any girl between 7 and 10 years of age can join the Brownie Guides if she can understand and is willing to make the Brownie Guide Promise:

I promise that I will do my best:
  To do my duty to God,
    To serve the Queen and help other people and
    To Keep the Brownie Guide Law.

The Brownie Guide Law is:
  A Brownie Guide thinks of others before herself and does a Good Turn every day.

Usually a Brownie will make her Promise after she has been with her Pack for several weeks. During the initial weeks she learns the meaning of the words and the commitment she is making.

Each Brownie pays a small pack subscription that covers the cost of equipment, badges, meeting hall and other incidentals, as well as an annual membership fee. A Brownie Guide's uniform is a light brown shirtwaist dress and knit cap, which shows her affiliation. She does not necessarily buy a new one: patterns for her uniform are available for the home seamstress, or she might be able to locate a second-hand uniform.

A Brownie is eligible to wear the Brownie Promise Badge after she has made her Promise at a special ceremony to which her parents or other adults are invited. The ceremony is also the first time she may wear her uniform, making the ceremony especially joyous.

Brownies are encouraged to take an active part in the religion of her family. That is the commitment she has made in her Promise Ceremony in saying, 'I promise to do my duty to God.' The Girl Guides Association respects the special requirements of each girl's faith as manifested in dress, diet, holy days and so on. Most Brownie packs are multi-faith, but others may be associated with a particular place of worship.

Each Brownie pack has a specific name and has between 18 and 24 members. Within the pack, members are

grouped into sixes, each of which is named after a folk-lore character, such as 'elves' or 'pixies'. Each six is self-governing to some degree, so each Brownie learns to make simple decisions that affect not only herself, but others as well. Membership in a six provides a small group of friends who take particular care of each other, and gives each girl a sense of belonging to something special.

Brownie packs normally meet one evening per week during regular school terms, but may enjoy special outings and events on weekends and holidays. The highlight of the year for Brownies is the Pack Holiday—when the pack goes away together. Brownies do not camp in tents, but enjoyment of the outing at their young age plants the seed for lifelong enjoyment of the outdoors.

GIRL GUIDES

Any girl between 10 and 15 years of age can become a Guide. She may have been a member of the Brownie Guides, but that is not a requirement. Every girl is welcome, whatever her faith or race, as long as she is able to understand and willing to make the Girl Guide Promise:

I promise that I will do my best:
To do my duty to God,
To serve the Queen and help other people and
To keep the Guide Law.

After she makes the Promise she is entitled to wear the Girl Guide Promise badge, and in so doing is trusted to keep the Girl Guide Law:

A Guide is loyal and can be trusted
A Guide is helpful
A Guide is polite and considerate
A Guide is friendly and a sister to all Guides
A Guide is kind to animals and respects all living things
A Guide is obedient
A Guide has courage and is cheerful in all difficulties
A Guide makes good use of her time
A Guide takes care of her own possessions and those of other people
A Guide is self-controlled in all she thinks, says and does.

To understand the activities she will be pursuing as a Guide, the girl first completes eight pre-promise Challenges. She also learns the meaning of the worlds of the Promise and the commitment she will be asked to make at her Promise Ceremony. The Promise Ceremony is attended by parents and others who want to celebrate the happy occasion, and usually takes place a couple of months after the girl has joined her regional Guide company.

Each Guide pays a small Company subscription and an annual membership subscription. She also wears a blue uniform which she has purchased or sewn and a colorful

To serve their country during World Wars I and II, the British Girl Guides performed a number of vital services, including doing duty as couriers (*at top*). In war or peace, well-prepared girls serve others, as this girl (*right*) shows in her service work involving elderly neighbors.

Above: These girls enter the World of Art. *Below:* An Air Force instructor oversees a World of Well-Being first aid exercise. One of this trio of hikers *(right)* wears a topsy-turvy t-shirt in the (sometimes rocky!) World of the Out-of-Doors.

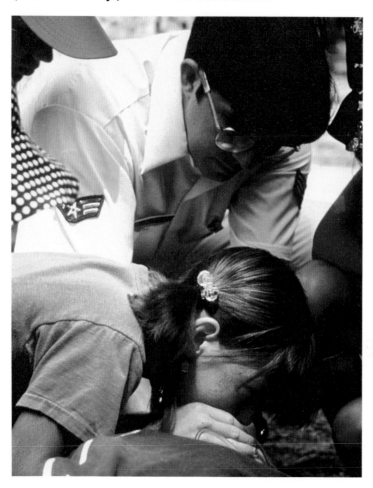

Left: **A Brownie troop at the park.** *Above:* **Guiders—adult volunteer leaders of Canadian Guide companies—training in 1925.** *Below:* **'Look wider' applies symbolically here: from the individual seashell to the vastness of the world ocean, a girl learns to broaden—and deepen—her experience.** *Overleaf:* **Girl Guides from Sweden (*left*) and the UK.**

neck scarf that indicates which region she lives in. A girl from North Yorkshire, for instance, wears a bright red neck scarf. Her uniform imparts a special sense of belonging to a movement, which has embraced sister Guides and Scouts from all over the world.

Most Guide Companies include girls from various faiths, but some companies are attached to a particular place of worship. Every Guide, whatever her faith, is encouraged to take an active part in the religion of her family. That is the commitment she has made at her Promise Ceremony when she says, 'I promise to do my duty to God.' The Girl Guides Association respects the special requirements of each girl's faith.

When a girl becomes a Guide, she becomes a member of a specific Guide Company which has its own specific name. Most companies have approximately 24 members. Smaller divisions of the Company are called Patrols and are named after flowers and birds. Six girls form a Patrol—a group of friends who take particular care of each other—which imparts a special sense of belonging to each member. Girls learn how to cooperate within their Patrols and Companies as well as learn how to lead, as each Guide learns to make decisions that affect herself and other people. Each Patrol has its own leader to represent them at the Patrol Leaders Council—which works with the adult leader to plan activities for the Company.

Each Guide is encouraged to set goals for herself, ranging from the Yellow Trefoil through Green and Red Trefoils, and finally to the Baden-Powell Trefoil, a Guide's highest award.

In 1933, international Roman Catholic Girl Guides and Guide personnel made a pilgrimage to the Vatican, where they were photographed *(above)* at the base of this obelisk dedicated to Pope Sixtus V. *Right:* These young ladies play basketball.

Specialist outdoor activities such as camping, fencing, horse riding and etc are supervised by qualified instructors.

Other activities come naturally to the Guide program—community work, fund raising or generally helping others. They are central to the Promise and Law. The Girl Guide motto is 'Be Prepared,' and Girl Guides strive to be ready to help wherever they can. In 1985, for instance, the Girl Guide/UNICEF Project raised 107,000 British pounds to show its care and dedication to helping others.

RANGER GUIDES

Girls who are from 14 to 18 years of age may become Ranger Guides. Any girl may become a Ranger Guide whether she has previously been a member of the Girl Guides Association or not. She may be of any race or religion and is welcomed into the Association. She is encouraged to take an active part in the religion of her family and community.

Ranger Guides, formed into Units, continue the program for girls that fosters the development of the best in girls by putting the principles of Guiding into practice. The age of Ranger Guides allows them greater creativity in the ways they can help others, and many projects that benefit other people and the community may be conceived and carried out by Ranger Guides.

Personal development at this age level may have taken a definite thrust in a certain direction, and membership in Ranger Guides encourages the development of special talents or skills. Ranger Guides come to realize that, by improving themselves they ultimately improve the world around them.

YOUNG LEADERS

A girl who is 15 to 18 years old may choose to develop her leadership talents as a Young Leader, working with a Brownie Pack or Guide Company to gain a certificate in youth leadership. Typically, a girl who participates in Young Leaders will have previously been a member of the Girl Guides Association, but even at this level that is not necessary. As long as she is willing to make the Girl Guide Promise, she may join the Association—one of the world's largest youth movements—embracing a worldwide membership of 8½ million in over 100 countries.

GIRL GUIDE FRIENDSHIP FUND

The Girl Guide Friendship Fund was launched in May 1964. Members of Girl Guiding in the United Kingdom, as individuals or groups, may contribute to this fund which is used to do Good Turns. The fund may be used within the United Kingdom to help the branch asso-

ciations of the Girl Guides Association, or overseas for major projects of independent associations of Girl Guides. The fund can, and has been used, to help in times of national disaster.

Administration of the fund is by the Girl Guide Friendship Fund Committee, which receives many requests for financial help from worthy charities. The Committee may choose to designate two or three projects as recipients of the Guiding World Appeal funds and the Christmas 'Good Turn' contributions. The Committee may also choose to give to individual charities, in what they call 'one-off' contributions from the general fund.

Money does not sit idle in the Girl Guide Friendship Fund. Every designated penny of every donation is used toward its particular Good Turn. Each donor may indicate which project is to receive her donation, and every donation is acknowledged and is issued a receipt by the Girl Guides Association. The expenses incurred in administering the fund, such as for postage or telephones, constitute about one percent of the annual donations—a percentage easily covered by the interest earned by donations on deposit during the period of each project.

Some of the countries helped by the Girl Guide Friendship Fund are Afghanistan, Antilles, Belize, Botswana,

Left, clockwise from top: **Experience makes future sailors; a young seamstress ties a rag rug; and a Brazilian girl smiles a sisterly hello.** *Below:* **These budding farmers work toward their animal interests badges.** *Overleaf:* **Parachute interest training.**

Brunei, Burundi, Cameroon, Chad, Chile, Ecuador, Ethiopia, El Salvador, Gabon, Kenya, Mexico, Nepal, Niger, Peru, Sri Lanka, Uganda and Zambia, among many others. The Friendship Fund has given lifeboats, hearing aids, agricultural equipment; guide dogs, hearing dogs, beds, riding equipment for physically handicapped people; talking books for the blind; and furnishings for day care centers. The literature from the Girl Guide Friendship Fund states with justifiable pride that it has helped to restore sight to babies in India; provided equipment for the deaf and blind in Sri Lanka, Malaysia and India; and adopted blind children and leprosy sufferers.

Money for the Friendship Fund is raised by Brownie packs, Guide patrols and companies, and Ranger Guides. As individuals or in groups, they may sponsor such money-raising activities as bazaars or rummage sales. Some may choose to donate from their own savings.

A small reserve is kept in the Fund, available for help without delay to sister Guides in times of national disaster. For example, a gift was sent immediately to Australia when the Girl Guide Friendship Fund learned of the devastating fires early in 1983 which destroyed campsites and other Guide property. Prompt help was given to the Jamaican Girl Guides when their headquarters were severely damaged by fire. When the enclosing wall at Sangam (one of the World Centers) was brought down by flood waters, financial aid was quickly on its way from the Disaster Fund reserve of the Girl Guide Friendship Fund.

GIRL GUIDING IN CANADA

The organization and activities of the Girl Guides of Canada are similar to those of Girl Scouts and Girl Guides in other countries. Its program helps girls become resourceful, responsible and happy individuals.

Canadian Girl Guides may pay small weekly fees to cover their local unit's expenses, and also pay an annual fee to the national organization. The national organization, whose official name is Girl Guides of Canada/Guides du Canada, administers the Girl Guide program from its headquarters in Toronto, Ontario. The organization is a member of WAGGGS, the international organization for Girl Guides and Girl Scouts. Among the ways the national organization serves its membership, is the publication of Girl Guide handbooks and *The Canadian Guider*, a magazine for adult leaders within the Girl Guide organization.

The first Canadian Guide Company was formed by Mrs A H Malcomson at St Catharines, Ontario and was registered with the British Girl Guide Office in 1910. Other companies were formed in Toronto and in Saskatchewan and Manitoba the same year. Canada was among the first countries to offer Girl Guiding, a movement born of the Boy Scout movement that spread quickly throughout the world. The Canadian Council of the Girl Guides Association was granted a charter by the Canadian Parliament in 1917.

The Girl Guides of Canada association charters its programs for use with girls of varying age levels. The Girl Guides of Canada are divided into six groups: Brownies, Guides, Pathfinders, Rangers, Junior Leaders and Cadets. The Girl Guide program is based on the Girl Guide Promise and a set of 10 Laws. Its educational program follows four 'Paths of Discovery': the home, the community, the out-of-doors and the world. Exploration of these paths is encouraged at each level of Guiding.

BROWNIES

Girls from six to nine years of age may join The Girl Guides of Canada as Brownies, organized into groups of approximately 24 girls, called packs. Leading a pack are two adult volunteers called a Brown Owl and a Tawny Owl.

Left: **Cross-country skiing is an enjoyable way to take a hike in the snowy woods, and these Guides are 'up for the fun.' Rules for Canadian Guide activities are not stringent, but the standard is that of enjoying games such as this three-legged race *(above)*, and engaging in such more complex, higher Guide level activities as ballet *(overleaf)* and other pursuits.**

A Brownie wears the official Brownie pin, in the shape of an elf, after she has made her Girl Guide Promise. Her uniform is not unlike Brownie uniforms everywhere. It is a brown dress, brown knee socks, brown belt, brown shoes and a white tie decorated with orange maple leaves.

The Brownie program has three levels: Pre-enrollment, Golden Bar and Golden Hand. Each level is increasingly difficult; a Brownie progressing through each level learns more about her home, her community and the out-of-doors in activities led by the Brown Owl and the Tawny Owl.

Brownies work to earn badges by developing their interests in such varied subjects as arts and crafts, sports, writing and music. In all their activities, Brownies learn to put into practice the ideals of Girl Guiding, which emphasize service to others.

Fitness in the World of Sports means fun and preparedness. These girls *(left)* receive scuba training by a qualified instructor, while other girls *(above)* get top-knotch advice as to how to avoid waterways and 'roughs' of all types.

GUIDES

A girl who is from 9 to 12 years of age may become a Guide. Guides form companies of no more than 24 girls, and each company is further divided into patrols of about six girls each. Each patrol has a Patrol Leader elected by her peers. Adult volunteer leaders are called Guiders. Patrol Leaders and Guiders together form the Court of Honor, the governing body of a company.

Guides wear a uniform consisting of a blue blouse and skirt, blue belt, blue knee socks, dark shoes and a white tie decorated with red maple leaves within a blue border. Guides also wear gold trefoil pins on their uniforms.

By working on projects in their local communities and in their homes, Guides develop skills and knowledge about the world close to them. They may also work in outdoor activities and can earn a variety of badges. Some of the subject areas that Guides pursue are astronomy, journalism, music and conservation.

PATHFINDERS

G irls 12 to 15 years old may join Pathfinder units. Each unit has about 15 girls and two adult leaders. Each unit has a Council composed of all its members and adult leaders, which discusses, plans and evaluates the activities for the unit. The Pathfinder program empha-

Above left: **Fitness seems to also be a part of these girls' 'bag.' These very directed young ladies** *(lower left)* **have their interest truly in focus. Preparedness and team effort in planning a trip is important to this troop** *(above).*

sizes challenge, adventure, shared leadership and shared experiences.

Pathfinders can work to earn five emblems available to them: the Outdoor emblem, Camping emblem, Community emblem, Home emblem and World emblem. To earn each emblem, Pathfinders must complete increasingly challenging tasks. Each Pathfinder works at her own pace as she furthers her interests along the Paths of Discovery.

RANGERS

Girls from 15 to 17 years of age may become Rangers. As Rangers they follow a program that calls for Investigation, Selection, Planning, Participation and Evaluation of activities. The program emphasizes individual development, even though Rangers plan group activities and projects and share leadership. At this age level, Rangers can also aim to participate in international events.

Rangers wear navy blue skirts, navy blue jackets and white blouses. For alternate activities, they may wear white turtleneck sweaters and navy blue trousers. Red maple leaves decorate their white scarves, and a blue-enameled trefoil pin further embellishes the Ranger uniform.

JUNIOR LEADERS

Most Junior Leaders are from 14 to 18 years old, and help adult leaders of Brownie packs in carrying out pack activities.

Junior Leaders wear navy blue skirts and white blouses similar to those worn by Guides, Rangers and Cadets.

The Junior Leader program was designed to appeal to girls who have never been members of other Girl Guide groups. After they have enjoyed their roles as Junior Leaders, they are encouraged to enter the Cadet program for leadership training.

CADETS

Cadets are from 15 to 17 years of age. They participate in a two-year training program for leadership. They learn by volunteering to assist adult leaders of Brownie packs, Guide companies, or Pathfinder units. They wear blue skirts, white blouses and yellow and white scarves.

Experience in the Cadet training program encourages young women to become leaders and to develop themselves to the best of their abilities. Some adults who trace their leadership training to Cadets have become professional staff persons for the Girl Guides of Canada. Many others who have achieved goals in different careers also trace their paths back to Cadets.

Above: This young woman seems to have found her direction in aviaculture. *Below, clockwise, starting at front:* Daisy and Junior Girl Scouts; an adult leader; Senior, Cadette and Brownie Girl Scouts. *At right:* These Juniors work to increase their already-impressive badge collections by following their interest in mime—which is not 'just clowning around.'

CONCLUSION

The opportunities for self development and the encouragement to set and reach goals have increased for young women and girls who are Scouts and Guides today. Today's Girl Scout or Girl Guide is as honorable, service oriented and fun loving as her predecessors were many years ago. Today's Girl Scout or Girl Guide, however, has different challenges to face, and her participation in the Scouting Movement helps prepare her to meet whatever challenges await her. She is encouraged to develop personal independence while maintaining her status as a team member. She strives to 'do her best' and to 'be prepared' as she tries to improve the world around her. She respects authority while reevaluating her own standards. She has a large task, but she's not alone. She has the support of the international sisterhood of Guides and Scouts in a bond no less strong than when it first surfaced. Girl Scouting today, composed of contemporary girls and led by modern adult leaders, prepares the girls not just for today, but for tomorrow.

Left: **These bird feeder-making Daisies seek to fatten our feathered friends. This Junior (*above*) seems the very epitome of Girl Scout Well-Being.** *Below:* **Enthusiasm makes for a heated race.** *Overleaf:* **Scouts and their leader enjoy canoeing.**

INDEX

Acknowledgements

Many thanks to Beverly Schlegel of the Muir Trail Girl Scout Council for all her help, and to Robin Gaines and Brownie Troop 565 for all their enthusiasm. Special thanks to Deborah Mason of Girl Scouts of the USA for her invaluable assistance in supplying the photographs.

Photo Credits

All photos supplied by Girl Scouts of the USA, except:
Action Photo Service: 40
AGS Archives: 41(top), 58 (top), 75
Bob Allen: 60 (bottom left)
Catholic Archdiocese of San Francisco: 43

Girl Guides Association (United Kingdom): 7, 9, 11, 17 (top and bottom), 18 (top and bottom), 19, 30, 77, 78, 79 (top and bottom), 80 (left and right), 82, 87 (top), 90
NASA: 110
© Carolyn Soto: 59 (bottom)
Pete Souza, The White House: 38
United States Air Force: 16 (bottom left), 58 (bottom left)
United States Department of Defense: 41 (bottom), 55, 59 (top)
Wyoming Travel Commission: 28
© Bill Yenne: 39 (top)

Far left: Dr Anna Fisher, a mission specialist on US space shuttle *Discovery* flight 51-A on 8 November 1984, is one of many accomplished women who have had Scouting experience. *Overleaf:* This Scout's unusual and rather chilly 'wider opportunity' is a diving expedition in Antarctica.